B R A N D S

B — Fermín Bohórquez

 Buendía

Francisco Chica

José Escobar

 Samuel Flores

Galache

G — Manuel González Martín

A — Miura

Antonio Urquijo

B R A N D S

M — San Mateo

 Pastejé

 Peñuelas

Xajay

 Zacatepec

Zotoluca

LA
FIESTA
BRAVA

LA FIESTA BRAVA

THE ART OF THE BULL RING

by Barnaby Conrad

———————— ILLUSTRATED ————————

HOUGHTON MIFFLIN COMPANY BOSTON

The Riverside Press Cambridge

1953

BOOKS BY BARNABY CONRAD

The Innocent Villa
Matador
La Fiesta Brava

The Riverside Press · CAMBRIDGE, MASSACHUSETTS

PRINTED IN THE U.S.A.

"Va por Bernabito,
Niño del Biberón!"

Acknowledgment

The author expresses thanks
to Katharine Bernard, who designed this book

CONTENTS

INTRODUCTION

1

On August 27, 1947, a multimillionaire and a bull killed each other in Linares, Spain, and plunged an entire nation into deep mourning. The bull's name was Islero, and he was of the Miura strain. The man's name was Manolete, and he was the essence of everything Spanish. His story is the embodiment of *la fiesta brava* (see glossary).

It's hard for Americans to understand why all this fuss about one bull-fighter. But he wasn't just a bullfighter to the Spaniards. He was their only national and international hero. Yet when he was killed, he died such a beautiful dramatic Spanish death that I swear, in spite of the great funeral, the week of national mourning, the odes, the dirges, the posthumous decorations by the government, that in his heart of hearts every Spaniard was glad that Manolete had died. They, the Spaniards themselves, murdered him.

He looked quixotic. Ugly in photos, cold and hard in the bull ring, he had tremendous magnetism, warmth, and gentle humor among his friends. Once, in Peru, I took a blasé American college girl to watch Manolete in the ceremony of preparing for a fight, though she protested she had no interest in a "joker who hurts little bulls."

"Excuse me, señorita, if I don't talk much," he said with his shy smile as they worried his thin frame into the skintight uniform, "but I am very scared."

After that he didn't say more than ten words to her. But she walked out of the room dazed. "That," she announced, "is the most attractive man in the world."

An hour later he had her weeping with emotion as he calmly let the horns of a giant Fernandini bull graze the gold braid on his costume time after time. The fear he spoke of was nowhere in evidence.

"To fight a bull when you are not scared is nothing," another bullfighter once said, "and to not fight a bull when you are scared is nothing. But to fight a bull when you are scared—that is something."

Manolete told me, "My knees start to quake when I first see my name on the posters and they don't stop until the end of the season."

But there was never any real end of the season for him. In 1945, for example, he fought ninety-three fights in Spain in six months, about one every other day. This meant body-racking travel, for he would fight in Barcelona one day, Madrid the next, and then maybe Lisbon the day after. He would snatch some sleep in the train or car and sometimes had to board a plane with his ring outfit still on. Then followed Mexico's season and Peru's season, and when he got through with those it was March again and time for the first fights in Valencia. It would be grueling even for a very strong man, and Manolete was frail to the point of appearing tubercular. Yet he kept driving, driving.

What, then, made him run? What made him The Best?

Money was the obvious thing. In his eight years as a senior matador he made approximately four million American dollars. In his last years he was getting as high as $25,000 per fight, about $400 for every minute he performed, and he could fight where, when, and as often as he liked. His yearly income was abetted by such things as a liqueur called Anís Manolete, dolls dressed in costume with his sad face on them, testimonials for cognac ads, songs about him, and a movie called *The Man Closest to Death*.

Yet it wasn't the money; people seldom risk their necks just for money. It was that he needed desperately to be someone—something great.

He was born Manuel Rodríguez in Córdoba, Spain, in 1917, in the heart of the bullfighting country. His great-uncle, a minor-league bullfighter, was killed by a bull, one of the dreaded Miura breed that years later was to kill Manuel. His mother was the widow of a great matador when she married Manuel's father, also a bullfighter. He began to go blind, kept fighting as long as he could distinguish the shape of the bull, and finally died in the poorhouse when Manuel was five years old.

The family was always hungry-poor. Manuel was a frail child, having had pneumonia when a baby, and could contribute little to his mother's support. But he started carrying a hod as soon as he was big enough to tote one.

His two sisters stood the hunger as long as possible, and then they started making money in a profession even older than bullfighting. This was the secret of the driving force behind Manuel. He never got over it. He resolved to make enough money somehow so that his family would never have to worry again, and to become an important enough person so that his sisters' shame would be blurred. Bullfighting is the only way in Spain for a poor boy to become great. "Matadors and royalty are the only ones who live well," they say. Young Manuel decided to become the greatest bullfighter who ever lived.

He was twelve and working as a plasterer's assistant on the Sotomayor ranch when he got his first chance. They raised fighting bulls, that special savage breed of beast originally found only on the Iberian peninsula, that can easily kill a lion or tiger. Little Manuel begged so persistently to be allowed to fight that finally the Sotomayors put him in the corral with a cape and a calf. On the opposite page (left) a lucky snapshot records the future immortal's first encounter with a toro bravo. Manuel, an awkward, skinny kid in short pants, was knocked down every time he went near the little animal. If the calf had had sharp horns instead of stubs, he would have been killed twenty times; instead he was just a mass of bruises by the time he limped out of the ring. He decided to go back to plastering.

But he couldn't stay away from the bulls. In the next few years he got out with the calves every time he could, even after he had been badly wounded, at thirteen, by a young bull.

There always are back-seat bullfighters around a ranch, and they told him some of the mistakes he was making. He learned fairly fast but he was no genius. He was awkward and tried to do the wrong kind of passes for his build. However, he was brave and took it so seriously that he finally

persuaded someone to give him a fight with small bulls in Córdoba's big plaza de toros, under the *nom de taureau* of Manolete, a diminutive of Manuel.

In his debut he was clumsy, but so brave and obviously trying so hard that the home folks applauded the sad-faced gawk. It was the greatest day of his life. Flushed with success, he and two other boys scraped their money together, formed a team called the Cordovan Caliphs, and set out to make their fortune. They wangled some fighting at night and in cheap fairs like the one in the photo above (right). Manolete was almost the comic relief of the outfit. The crowds would laugh at his skinny frame, made more awkward by the fancy passes he was trying. His serious, homely face and his earnestness made it all the funnier.

"He looks as dreary as a third-class funeral on a rainy day," they'd say. But they couldn't laugh at the way he killed. He was so anxious to do well that when it came time to dispatch his enemy, Manolete would hurl himself straight over the lowered head, the horn missing his body by inches, to sink the sword up to the hilt between the shoulders.

"He's going to get killed that way someday," said the experts.

His career, if you could call it that at this point, was interrupted by his being drafted into the army. After his discharge a year later he resumed fighting without the other two Caliphs. Then came the turning point in his life, for Camará spotted him.

José Flores Camará, a bald, dapper little man of thirty-five with omnipresent dark glasses, might have become the greatest bullfighter of all time except for one thing: he was a coward. He displayed more grace and knowledge of bull psychology than anyone had ever seen before. He had the build and he knew all about the different fighting habits of bulls and the rest of the complicated science of tauromachy. The only thing he couldn't do was keep his feet from dancing back out of the way when the bull charged, which is the most important thing in bullfighting.

When he saw Manolete gawking around a small-town ring, he knew that here was someone who could be everything that he had failed to be. With his expert eye he saw what the crowd didn't, that the boy wasn't really awkward, but that he was trying the wrong passes for his build and personality. Camará figured that with his brains and Manolete's blood they could really go places. He signed up the astonished young man for a long, long contract.

Camará remade Manolete. He took him out to the ranches and showed him what he was doing wrong. He made him concentrate on just the austere classic passes, none of the spinning or cape-twirling ones. With the cape he showed him how to do beautiful slow verónicas, finishing with a half-verónica. It was the only pass, of the dozens that exist, that Manolete would ever do again with the cape. With the small muleta cape used with the sword, Camará let him do only four passes. He showed him how to hold himself regally, how to give the classic passes with a dignity never before seen in the ring.

When Camará thought Manolete was ready, he launched his protégé. It took a little while for people to appreciate what they were witnessing, but soon they came to realize that here was a revolutionary, a great artist. His repertory was startlingly limited, but when he did the simple verónica the cape became a live thing in his hands, and the easy flow of the cloth, the casual way it brought the bull's horns within a fraction of an inch of his legs, was incredibly moving. Heightening the effect was the serious mien and the cold face, which gave a feeling of tragedy every time he went into the ring.

No one laughed at him now. Camará had made a tragic genius out of a clown. And always the nervous little man with his dark glasses was behind the fence while his protégé was out with the bull, watching every move and saying: "Careful, Manolo, this one will hook to the left," or "Take him on the other side, he has a bad eye," or "Fight him in the center, he swerves when he's near the fence." And Manolete kept learning and learning.

If his first year was successful, his second was sensational. It seemed as though Spain had just been waiting for his kind of fighting. His honest and brave style showed up the fakery that the cape-twirlers had been foisting

upon the public. In 1939 he took "the alternative" and became a senior matador, fighting older and larger bulls. From then on his rise was dizzying, for every fight and every season seemed better than the last one.

By 1946 he was the king of matadors and Mexico beckoned with astronomical contracts, the highest prices ever paid a bullfighter. Spectators thought they were lucky to get a seat for $100 for his first fight in Mexico City. It was the greatest responsibility a matador ever had, and he gave them their money's worth, although he was carried out badly wounded before the fight was half over. He came to as they were carrying him to the ring infirmary, shook off the people who tried to stop him, and lurched back into the ring to finish the bull, before collapsing.

After he recovered he went on to fight all over Mexico and South America. When I saw him in Lima he was exhausted. Most bullfighters can give a top performance one day and then get away with a few safe, easy ones. But not Manolete. To preserve his fabulous reputation he had to fight every fight as though it were his first time in the Madrid plaza.

But the machine was wearing down. Though he was only twenty-nine, he looked forty. He was drinking a lot; not mild Spanish wine but American whisky. His timing was beginning to go off. I remember once in Peru he took nine sword thrusts to kill a bull, and he left the ring with tears running down his cheeks.

Even Camará, who enjoyed having his wallet filled through risks taken by someone else, thought it was time to quit. But the public makes an idol and then it tires of what it has made and it destroys the idol. When Manolete returned to Spain and announced that he was going to retire, he found he had slipped from public grace. The people were now saying that he dared to fight only small bulls and that this new young Luis Miguel Dominguín

PAGE 8

5

was better and braver. Manolete had been on top too long. They wanted someone new. They amused themselves by changing the words of the once popular eulogizing song, "Manolete," to: "Manolete, you couldn't even handle a robust field mouse if confronted by one in the bathroom."

"Quit," Camará advised him. "Quit," said Luis Miguel, who would then be cock of the roost. "Quit," said the other bullfighters, who then wouldn't look so clumsy and cowardly.

Manolete had too much pride to quit under fire. He said he would have one last season, just a few short months, with the largest bulls in Spain, and fighting with any fighters the promoters wished to bill him with. He wanted to retire untied and undefeated.

His first fight was in Barcelona, and the critics said he had never been greater. Then Pamplona, and he was even better than at Barcelona. It looked as though everyone was wrong, that he was in his prime.

Then, on July 16, he was wounded in Madrid. The wound wasn't serious, but he left the hospital too soon to go on a vacation in the mountains with Antonia, his mistress. He began fighting again long before he should have; it was as though he were afraid that if he missed any of these last contracts there would always be some people who would remain unconvinced that he was still The Best.

The next fights were not good. He just wasn't up to it physically, and he wasn't helping himself by the way he was drinking. He would stay up all night with a bottle of whisky, not go to bed, and try to fight the next afternoon. They say he drank because of Antonia, because he knew she was a girl "of a bad style" and a gold digger, but that he loved her and couldn't break off with her and hated himself for loving her. A friend of his said, "She dragged poor Manolo through the Street of Bitterness with her cheapness."

Also the crowd's new attitude toward him was intolerable, not because of egotism but because of his professional pride. Now they were always prone to applaud the other matadors more, no matter how close Manolete let death come.

"They keep demanding more and more of me in every fight," he complained to me. "And I have no more to give." People want heroes, need heroes, but the Manolete myth had outgrown the real Manolete, and the people were angry at him instead of at themselves for having created it.

Then came August 27 and the fight in Linares. It was extremely important to him that he be good this afternoon. First, because it was near his home town; second, because Luis Miguel Domínguín was on the same program; third, because the bulls were Miuras, the famous "bulls of death" that have killed more men than any other breed in existence. People claimed that Manolete was scared of Miuras and had always avoided fighting them.

Since it was midsummer and the sun shines till nine in Andalusia, the fight didn't begin until six-thirty. It began, like any other of his fights—the stands jammed with mantilla-draped señoritas and men with the broad-brimmed sombreros cocked over one eye. There was an excitement in the air because of the Miuras and the rivalry between Domínguín and Manolete. The stylish gypsy Gitanillo de Triana completed the bill.

Gitanillo did well by the first bull and received applause and handker-chief-waving, which meant the audience wanted him to be granted an ear of the dead bull as a token of a good performance. But the president of the arena was hard to please and refused to grant it.

The second bull was Manolete's. It was dangerous and unpredictable, but Manolete was out to cut an ear. He made the animal charge back and forth in front of him so closely and gracefully that even his detractors were up out of their seats, yelling. But when it came time to kill, he missed with the first thrust. The second dropped the bull cleanly and the crowd applauded; but he had lost the ear; they were demanding perfection today.

The trumpet blew, and it was Luis Miguel's turn. This was an important fight to him also. He wanted to show up the old master in his own province. He wanted to show them who could handle Miuras better than anyone in the world.

He strode out into the arena, good-looking, smug, twenty years old. Manolete was through—here was the new idol, here was the king of the rings!

He had the crowd roaring on the first fancy, twirling passes with the big cape. He put in his own banderillas superbly, to win more applause. With the muleta, the little cape that is draped over the sword for the last part of the fight, he unfurled all of his crowd-pleasing tricks, dropping to his knees for two passes and even kissing the bull's forehead at one moment. He lined the bull up, thrust the sword in between the withers halfway up to the hilt, and the animal sagged down dead. The crowd cheered and waved their handkerchiefs until the president granted Domínguín an ear.

Manolete had watched the entire performance from the passageway, with no change of expression. Those tricks and cape twirls were not his idea of true bullfighting. He would show the crowd what the real thing was if it killed him.

After Gitanillo's mediocre performance with his second animal, Manolete saw the toril gate swing open and the last bull of his life came skidding out of the tunnel. It was named Islero. The moment Camará saw it hooking around the ring, he sucked in his breath and said to Manolete: "Malo—bad, bad. It hooks terribly to the right." That is a dread thing, for a matador must go over the right horn to kill. "Stay away from this one, chico!"

But Manolete was determined to give the best performance of his life. He caught the collar of the cape in his teeth and held it while he got the big magenta cloth right in his hands. Then he slid through the opening in the fence and called the bull.

"Toro, hah, toroooo!" he called in his deep voice, holding the cape out in front of him and shaking it.

The animal wheeled at the voice, its tail shot up, and it charged across the ring. As it reached the cloth the man did not spin or swirl the cape around him or dance about the way that Luis Miguel had done. He merely planted his feet and swung the cape slowly in front of the bull's nose, guiding the great head with the tantalizing cloth so that the left horn went by his legs ten inches away. Without moving his feet, he took the bull back in another charge and the right horn stabbed six inches away from his thighs. Five more perfect classic verónicas, each closer than the other, finishing with a half-verónica that was so close that the bull's neck hit him and nearly knocked him off balance. He turned his back on the bewildered animal and looked up at the crowd that was cheeringly deliriously.

With the muleta cape, his forte, he worked in even closer, until the crowd was shouting, "No, no!" Camará was shouting with them, for Manolete was passing the animal just as closely on the dangerous right side as the left. But the man didn't pay any attention. He did the Pass of Death and his own pass, the dangerous "manoletina." He did fifteen suicidal "natural" passes, the one where the sword is taken out of the cape and only the limp bit of rag is used to divert the bull's charge away from the body. Then he did his famous trademark—the fantastic pass where he looked disdainfully away from the bull up into the stands as the animal thundered by. It seemed as though the bull couldn't miss, but it did. By now the crowd was hoarse from cheering the domination that the man had acquired over the beast.

It was time to kill. As he was lining up the Miura so that the feet would be together and the shoulder blades open, Camará and his banderilleros were yelling: "Stay away from him, man! Off to the side and get away quick!"

But Manolete had to finish this one right. He wasn't going to spoil the performance by running off to the side and stabbing it in the lungs. He was going to head in straight, get the sword in, give the bull a fair shot at him, and hope to God it wouldn't hook to the right.

He stood in front of the Miura, sighted down the blade, rose on the toes of one foot, and as the bull lunged forward, Manolete hurled himself straight over the lowered right horn. The sword was sinking in, the horn cutting by him. But suddenly the bull wrenched its head to the right and drove the horn deep into the man's groin. Manolete was flung high into the air, trying to fight the horn out of his body, and then was slammed to the sand. The bull spiked at him twice on the ground and then staggered, choked, and flopped over dead, the sword up to the red hilt between its shoulder blades.

The pool of blood on the sand told them the man was mortally wounded. Camará and the banderilleros picked up the unconscious form and rushed him down the passageway to the ring infirmary. He regained consciousness on the operating table and gasped weakly, "Did it die?"

"Sí, chico, sí," said Camará, tears raining down his cheeks.

"It died and they didn't give me anything?" Manolete said, trying to raise himself from the table.

"They gave you everything, Matador," said a banderillero, putting his cigarette between the wounded man's lips. "Everything—both ears and tail."

He smiled and lay back.

At five in the morning he moaned, "Doctor, I can't feel anything in my right leg." The doctor assured him he would be well in no time. Then, "Doctor, I can't feel anything in my left leg." He gave a cry and said, "I can't see!" and he was dead.

An old banderillero, staring at the corpse, said dully, "They kept demanding more and more of him, and more was his life, so he gave it to them."

There is the story, then, of a brave tragic figure. His was a dramatic storybook life. He was a man who placed his profession—a strange ancient-modern art—above everything else.

This book is about that art.

LA
FIESTA
BRAVA

THE ORIGINS

Cossío, in his monumental work *Los Toros,* warns: "He who would understand the purpose of this book should take into consideration that the festival of bullfighting is not merely a pastime debatable from moral, pedagogical, esthetic, and sentimental points of view, but must accept that it is a fact of profound meaning in the Spanish way of life and possessing roots so deep and extensive that there is no social or artistic activity, from the language to industry or commerce, where traces of it cannot be found."

We know that ancient peoples, such as the Cretans, practiced games with bulls, leaping over their backs and doing other acrobatic tricks, but the actual fighting of bulls finds its origins in Spain. The reason for this is *Bos taurus ibericus:* the bull indigenous only to the Iberian Peninsula.

Most people do not realize that the fighting bull is a race apart from the domestic animal. The savage toro bravo and the placid toro manso are as different as a cobra and a gopher snake. The fighting bulls are born to fight, never trained, tortured, or starved as people will try to have you believe. This species of bull—El Toro Bravo or El Toro de Lidia—is the only animal suitable for the arena. The animals fought in the Latin American countries which practice bullfighting—Mexico, Peru, Venezuela, Colombia, Ecuador, and Bolivia—are descendants of Spanish stock.

There are domestic cattle in Spain, of course, but the toro bravo is scrupulously kept pure. He has been bred for centuries for one purpose and one purpose only—to kill men and horses.

Perhaps his ancestor was the bison below, right, sketched by a primitive man on the walls of the caves of Altamira. And perhaps the first bullfight took place when a caveman had to defend himself against a wounded bisonte by flinging his skin garment at it to distract it.

For centuries herds of fierce toros bravos roamed wild over Spain, and the Romans imported them for their Colosseum orgies.

Though we are told that Julius Caesar himself tried a hand at taurine games in ancient Sevilla, it was the Arabs, not the Romans, who gave real

PAGE 14

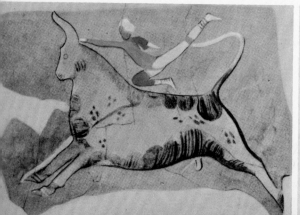
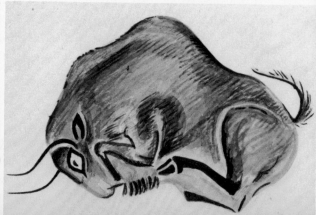

impetus to bullfighting, following their victory over the Goths. It began as a sporting chase after herds of the vicious toros bravos, the horsemen lancing the animals as the bulls charged at them.

Supposedly, the celebrated cavalier, El Cid Campeador, was the first person to participate in organized bull festivals in enclosures. This would be around 1090. The sport consisted of a skillful horseman killing a wild bull with a lance while guiding his horse so as to avoid injury both to his mount and himself. (This is still the principle behind modern rejoneo, or Portuguese-style fighting. See page 158).

Bullfighting quickly became very popular and for centuries rich Moors and Christians, nobles and even kings, practiced it, no feast day being complete without the spectacle. Bullfighting became so popular and the fatalities so numerous that Pope Pius V issued a Papal Ban in 1567 threatening excommunication to all Christians killed while participating in the spectacle. But it did little to deter the Spaniards' passion for what the Greeks called *tauromachia*—bull-combatting—and the proclamation was eventually canceled.

Isabella, and various kings after her, tried to discourage the nobles from risking their lives at this pursuit, but it took a Frenchman, Philip V, the first Bourbon king of Spain, to discourage the grandees. It was not only that they feared their monarch's displeasure; it was also because the common people, fighting the animals on foot with capes, began to overshadow the nobles' feats.

In 1700 a carpenter named Francisco Romero invented the muleta, a flaglike cloth whose handling is the most important phase of modern bull-fighting. He also was the first man to kill a bull face to face. Romero's grandson Pedro became director of the School of Tauromachy in Sevilla, which was created by King Ferdinand VII.

From then on bullfighting became more and more refined, each great figure adding his personal touch to the spectacle, each decade seeing subtle innovations, until it has arrived at the intricate science that is the modern corrida. And along with the development of the art went the development of the bull itself.

THE BULL

The *sine qua non* of bullfighting is a beautiful, lethal wild beast. It has been bred for fighting for four centuries, until now it is the most perfect living instrument for killing that man can devise. Faster than race horses for the first few hundred feet, they can turn more quickly than polo ponies. Characteristic is the large hump of tossing muscle—the morillo—which swells when the bull is enraged, the small hoofs, and the long silky tail. Usually smaller than their domestic brethren, they are infinitely more agile.

PAGE 16

The animals are raised on ranches that dedicate themselves exclusively to raising bulls for the arena. A fighting bull costs approximately $1000, and over 4000 of them are killed in an average year in Spain. Some of the principal ganaderías—or bull farms—of Spain are Miura, Urquijo (formerly Murube), Buendía, Concha y Sierra, Galache, Pablo Romero, Conde de la Corte, Tulio Vásquez, Domecq (formerly Veragua), and Villamarta. In Mexico the names which most excite the aficionados are the ranches of La Punta, San Mateo, Piedras Negras, La Laguna, and Pastejé.

Animals from each of these ranches have distinguishing characteristics. Certain bulls will have a tendency to toss their heads up halfway through a pass, and bullfighters come to expect that and guard against it. From another ranch they will have a tenacious quality which causes them to stick with a fallen torero like the one above and ignore the capes of those trying to save him. Still others are fine for the opening capework but "arrive like lead" for the final third of the fight. The bull breeder has a much harder task than the breeder of horses; while the race horse needs only speed, the fighting bull must also be bred for size, type of horn, and, most important, temperament and courage.

The best bull is the bravest bull, one that charges hard upon the slightest provocation. It is the type of animal that most pleases the crowd, the breeder, and the toreros. Every bull is given a number, which is branded big on its side, and a name, and it is carefully watched and nurtured as an individual from the time it is born. Yet no one can be sure whether it will put up a brave or cowardly performance until it is actually in the ring. The only indication the breeder has is the bull's lineage and its behavior during the testing.

The tienta or tentadero—the bravery test—is given the animal when it is approximately two years old. Both the bulls and the heifers are tested, since breeders maintain that a fighting bull gets his size from his father but his heart from his mother. One test is el derribo, or "the knocking down."

A young animal is cut from the herd in an open field and is pursued by two horsemen carrying blunt-tipped lances known as garrochas. When the pole catches the calf just right at the base of his tail, it is spilled end over end. If it gets off the ground fighting mad and pursues the horse, the breeder assumes it is not cowardly and records it in his notebook.

Much more conclusive evidence, however, comes from the testing ring. Here the young bulls and heifers are let into the small arena one at a time with a picador, who is mounted on a padded horse. The animals immediately sense that they are in this enclosure to fight, and they need no encouragement to charge the horse ferociously; they come in buscando guerra—"looking for war"—from the first moment. The picador pricks the animal in the withers with a sharp-tipped lance, and the performance is judged by how long it stays banging its stubby horns against the horse in spite of the annoying lance and how quickly and how many times it recharges. The heifers proving exceptionally brave are slated for motherhood. The young bulls that attack the picador relentlessly are scheduled for a destiny in the arena; the others are discards, and the butcher shop is their end. The breeder indicates their fate by calling out to the vaqueros "toro" if he thinks the calf has put up a brave performance and "buey" (steer) if it is to be castrated.

The male calves are not caped at tientas because they have good memories and would remember the experience when they came to enter the big

PAGE 18

arena years later. The corrida is based upon the premise that the bull is encountering a dismounted man for the first time in its life. A bull which had been caped extensively when young might come into the ring realizing that the cape was a ruse and that the man behind it was his true enemy. Bulls are not particularly smart, but they have good memories.[1]

Many stories are told of bull's memories. The immortal Joselito once drew a bull which refused to charge the picador on his white horse. Judged cowardly, it was ordered from the ring. But Joselito decided that the reason it didn't charge was because it remembered being pic-ed by a man on a white horse at its "trial" when it was a calf. He had the picador change to a dark horse and the bull charged immediately.

The heifers are worked over intensively with cape and muleta, both as part of their testing and to provide practice for the men. A tienta is always the occasion for a party and the guests include gentlemen toreros, professionals, and aspirant matadors, all eager to show off their capework.

Below, left, Juan Belmonte, the father of modern bullfighting and now a prominent breeder of bulls, studies a two-year-old cow after a series of passes. Fighting heifers are virtually udderless and resemble young bulls in conformation. They are trickier to fight, but not because "unlike bulls they keep their eyes open." Contrary to legend, neither bulls nor cows shut their eyes when they charge. (A glance at some of the photographs will prove this—see pages 45 and 118.) Young cows *are* harder to fight, but it is because of being lighter and slighter of build that they can turn and swerve a little quicker than bulls; of course they are less murderous than the powerful males. At the right, the author practices a right-hand muleta pass with a two-year-old heifer in Juan Belmonte's private ring on his ranch in Sevilla.

[1] In a lecture, I once remarked that bulls have very small brains for their size, actually not much larger than a baseball. Whereupon Sinclair Lewis bellowed indignantly from the audience, "And just how big is a bullfighter's brain?"

PAGE 19

After a bull's testing he is let alone to grow big and rugged; the regulations state that for his one and only ring appearance, he must weigh over 900 pounds and be four years old. The bulls learn to use their horns by fighting among themselves as they are below and sometimes the ganadero, the breeder, toughens them by making them walk miles every day for their feed. A constant vigil is kept on the animals destined for the ring, to see that young aspirants don't sneak onto the ranch and practice their capework on these animals which should go into the ring limpios—clean. But every Spanish boy dreams of being a torero, and many of them, made brave by dreams of being another Belmonte or Manolete, have sneaked into the fields by moonlight and ruined good bulls by their clumsy attempts at caping. And many have gasped out their lives lying bloody and torn in the high grass while their frightened companions ran to the ranch house for help.

Finally the day for which all the other days have been a preparation arrives for the fighting bull. Perhaps it is a big fight, like the Corrida de la Prensa or La Policía in Madrid or the first of the Feria fights in Sevilla. If the bull ring is reasonably close to the ranch the six bulls are driven across country to it. The black and white animals in the photograph at the right are the cabestros, the trained steers with bells around their necks who are used to keep the bulls calm. Bulls have a strong herd instinct and when in a group are usually quiet and manageable. However, bulls being taken to the ring have been known to break from the herd and attack automobiles

PAGE 20

and cyclists. Once a bull in Sevilla turned over a car with one jerk of its powerful neck muscle, and then repeatedly drove its sharp horns through the metal body. The terrified driver scrambled out and sprinted for the protection of a cottage. The bull overtook him before he could slam the door and crashed into the house with the victim spiked on one horn. There was only one person at home, an old woman, and the bull killed her before the Guardia Civil could arrive to shoot the animal through a window.

PAGE 21

17

Generally the bulls are not herded but shipped to the plaza de toros in heavily reinforced crates called cajones. The animals are delivered to the back of the bull ring for the desencajonamiento—the de-boxing.

In 1929 during a de-boxing at the Madrid arena a bull somehow escaped. It made its frightening way down the great boulevards of the city, goring several people and finally holding a large crowd at bay on the Gran Via, Madrid's Broadway. A retired bullfighter, Diego Fortuna, happened to come along at that moment. He took off his overcoat and caped the animal into the middle of the street away from the terrified crowd, keeping the bull distracted until his wife returned with his sword. After he had killed it with one thrust, the crowd insisted on giving him the ears and tail and the Spanish government awarded him the Cruz de la Beneficencia, its highest civilian decoration.

Once out of the shipping crate, the bull is lured, sometimes by a cloth dangled on the end of a rope, into the corral where it will spend the few days before the fight. They are fed well and kept quiet. Visitors are usually allowed to come to see the animals—for a small price to the corral keeper—but they must not attract the attention of the bulls or excite them. However, occasionally the animals' fighting instincts will be aroused, as

PAGE 22

18

19

in the case of the two bulls below. The bull on the ground is already dead and the killer dropped a few moments later from the tremendous impact of the initial charge.

At noon the day of the fight, the sorteo—or drawing for the bulls—takes place. Matadors seldom attend the sorteo, preferring to send their number one banderillero instead. The representatives of the matadors pair off the bulls in the fairest fashion —that is, the three worst with the three best, the largest and/or most dangerously horned animals with the ones that are smaller and/or have less wide horns. Each pair's numbers are then written on a piece of cigarette paper and dropped in a hat. After the drawing the animals are lured into separate stalls, where they rest in the semidarkness until the fateful trumpet signals their entry into the ring.

People will tell you the bulls are kept in the dark so that they will be blinded by the sun and confused in the arena. This, of course, is not true. Bullfighting is based on the bull's following a cape, and the better he sees the better it is for the bullfighter. He is kept in the dark so that when the toril gate is opened he will head immediately for the light and the arena.

PAGE 23

20

21

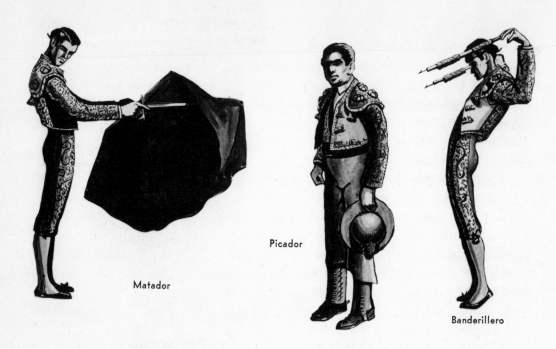

Matador

Picador

Banderillero

THE PERFORMERS

Meanwhile the performers who are going to take on these bulls are trying to rest in their homes or hotel rooms. Of the three classifications of toreros (never toreadors, an archaic term popularized by Bizet), the most nervous are the matadors, for they are the stars of the show.

Three matadors make up the customary program, killing two bulls apiece. Usually they are between 19 and 30 years old if they are full-fledged matadors, younger if they are novilleros. Always clean-shaven, they are the only performers who handle the sword or go bareheaded in the arena. There are only about thirty active first-class matadors in the world. For an afternoon's performance a top "sword" (espada) will receive the equivalent of $5000. Manolete was reputedly paid $35,000 for a single fight in Mexico in 1945. Out of this the matador must pay his traveling expenses, his manager, his sword boy, his cuadrilla—his five ring assistants—and for his costumes and capes.

Every matador has three banderilleros who are in and around the ring for one purpose: to protect the matador and to help him look good. They place banderillas—the darts—if the matador doesn't place them himself, and they cape the bull into position for the matador, but they do not try to shine themselves unless they want to get fired. Banderilleros (or peones, as they are sometimes called) are usually older men, often onetime matadors who early in the game saw they did not have the necessary guts and skill to be matadors and joined a successful "sword's" cuadrilla. A banderillero receives around $50 a fight, considerably less than what his employer makes but completely fair when the risks of the two professions are compared. While the matador's costume may be brocaded with silver, or gold, the banderillero must wear only silver or black patterns on the colored silk.

Each matador has two picadors—horsemen equipped with eight-foot lances called varas. Hefty men, who receive less than the banderilleros, they are usually the villains of the piece. It is they who must punish the neck muscles of the bull to prepare it for the last third of the fight. Bullfight crowds save their special invectives and mother-insults for bad jobs of pic-ing. Rarely does one hear applause for the hapless picador.

Even bullfights are unionized, and each category of torero belongs to a protective sindicato.

The day of the fight, the matador tries to rest as much as possible. He has probably flown or driven into town the night before after a corrida in another city. It is not unusual for a matador to fight in Lisbon one day and the next in Barcelona, at the other extreme of the Peninsula. Juan Belmonte fought an incredible 109 corridas in 180 days back in 1919, a record that stood until Litri broke it with 114 in 1950. The traveling alone that a torero must do is exhausting without the added emotional and physical drain of the performing.

The matador usually stays in bed until noon, at which time he has coffee. On corrida days he eats lightly or not at all so that he can be operated on immediately if he is gored. The chances of this are good. It has been estimated that 10 per cent of bullfighters are killed in the ring, 13 per cent are crippled, and 40 per cent are wounded at least twenty times in their career. (This percentage of deaths seems exaggerated, as there have been only ten top matadors killed in the last twenty years, but it is the fatalities of obscure young fighters in small towns which swell the figure.)

Carnicerito de México had over fifty wounds which were pronounced "fatal" by the ring doctors; the last one took. He worshiped Manolete and was haunted by his death, predicting that he would die as the Spaniard had done. This he did a few weeks later, in the same manner as his idol and gasping out the same dying sentences.

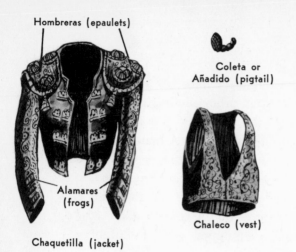

Hombreras (epaulets)

Coleta or
Añadido (pigtail)

Alamares
(frogs)

Chaleco (vest)

Chaquetilla (jacket)

THE DRESSING

Camisa (shirt)

Corbatín
(tie)

Montera (hat)

Faja (sash)

Zapatillas (slippers)

Machos (tassels)

Taleguilla (pants)

Esclavina
(collar)

Capa de Paseo
(dress cape)

The somber ritual of dressing a bull-fighter in his intricate traje de luces (suit of lights) takes about an hour and a half. Besides the matador's manager and sword boy there are usually a dozen or so people wandering in and out, wishing him well in hushed tones or asking him to autograph paper fans and photographs. Most bullfighters want people in the room to distract them from the sinking fear-feeling that they all get.

Below, Manolete wraps his toes before pulling on the two pairs of white cotton stockings and the outer pair of pink silk. Afterwards comes the underwear and the taleguilla— the pants. In the next photograph, the Mexican matador Luis Procuna manages a nervous smile at a visitor while his machos are being tied.

22

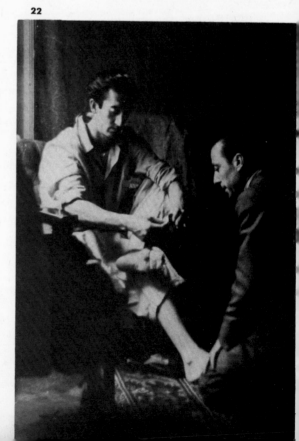

The modern traje de luces (lower right) differs very little from the costume of 125 years ago. Real pigtails have not been worn, however, since the independent and unpredictable Juan Belmonte one day decided to cut his off; for over 25 years the false coleta has been used. Weighing about 25 pounds, a "suit of lights" costs $200 in Spain, $400 in Mexico, and would run about $2000 to duplicate in America, and a top matador must have about eight for a season. The silk may be any color, but the heavy lamé which incrusts it will be gold, silver, or black. Dress capes can cost $1000. The most famous taurine tailors are Santiago Pelayo in Madrid and Manfredi in Sevilla, and most Mexican matadors order their uniforms from them.

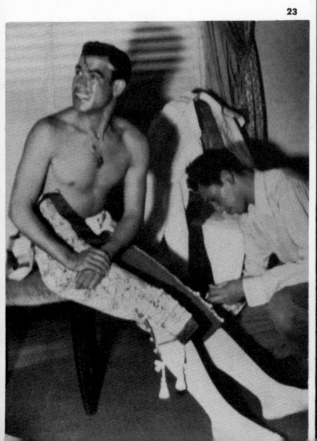

"TO THE BATTLE!"

When the matador is dressed he prays in front of the candles and triptychs of his special Virgin, on the bureau, asking for protection and luck. Then he will say something like: "A la lucha!" (to the battle) or "A la plaza," and the entourage will start for the plaza de toros.

Bullfights are the only functions in Spain and Latin America which begin on time. Early in the season they will begin around four o'clock, but because of the late blistering summer sun of Andalucía it is not unusual for fights to begin at seven-thirty.

There is a tense excitement in the air now. As Richard Ford wrote a hundred years ago: "Nothing, when the tide is full, can exceed the gaiety and sparkle of a Spanish public going, eager and dressed in their best, to the fight." If the fight is held during Fair time, many of the women will be wearing mantillas and the men the flat-topped sombreros cordobeses. "A los toros!" friends call back and forth to each other exuberantly, "To the fights!" (Bullfights, generally and specifically, are referred to as "the bulls" in Spanish.)

As the bullfighters drive through the streets in cars and sometimes carriages, like these picadors, the crowds that are already milling toward the ring cheer them. Notice the metal guards, called "monas," on the picadors' right legs.

PAGE 28

The first thing to know about bullfighting is that the audience is not going to the plaza de toros to watch the cruelty to the animals, the way people attended bull-baiting in England as recently as the 1890's. There is cruelty there, but that is not why they are going.

If the death and suffering of animals was all they wanted to enjoy they could visit their local abattoir for free, instead of paying as much as $20 for a seat at the bull ring. Nor do they go to the plaza de toros for the same reasons they attend prizefights or cockfights.

The eminent British bull critic John Marks writes: "The bullfight is sometimes condemned as the particularly depraved combination of a spectator-sport and a blood-sport, in which the gloating witness runs no personal risk. The accusation is unjust. The bullfight audience takes neither part nor pleasure in causing pain to the victims of the fiesta, whose sacrifice is not contrived as an end in itself, to provide selfish amusement, but solely as a means to conjure up visions of movement and colour, and to excite the sublime tragic emotion which Aristotle defined as pity mixed with fear."

The aficionados go for one reason: to see the almost-death of the matadors. Hence the men who most gracefully maximize the death chance to themselves within the aesthetic ritual become known as the best bullfighters.

The second elementary thing to bear in mind is that bullfighting is not a sport. It is never referred to as "un deporte" by Spaniards or Latin Americans, but always as "un arte"; the daily bull information and events are not chronicled under the sporting section in newspapers but rather in a special section entitled "Los Toros" or "Noticias Taurinas." It is an art. It is a spectacle. It is a tragedy. But not a sport.

THE PLAZA

There are over 400 bull rings in Spain alone. Half of these accommodate less than 5000 people, like the picturesque little plaza de toros in Chinchón, near Aranjuez, shown in the photograph on the following page. (The men are not dressed in the usual traje de luces, because this is a small "festival" fight. Usually for charity, festivals feature young animals. There are no picadors, and the toreros perform free. The men wear the traje corto costume, consisting of high boots, tight pants, short bolero jacket, and either the broad-brimmed sombrero cordobés or a golf cap, called la gorra.)

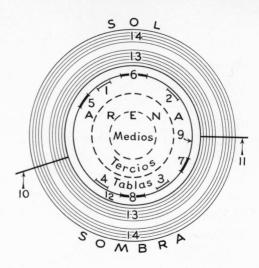

Sol—sunny side   Sombra—shady side

1,2,3,4—Burladeros. Protective wooden shields in front of openings in the fence which are large enough for a man to slide in and out of but too small for the bull.

5—Puerta del Toril. Door to the tunnel from which the bull enters.

6—Puerta de Cuadrillas. Where the bullfighters first enter the ring and where the dead bulls are dragged out.

7—Puerta de la Enfermería. Door to the infirmary.

8—Puerta de Picadores. Gate used by picadors to enter and leave ring.

9—Barrera. The wooden fence enclosing the arena.

10,11—División Entre Sol y Sombra. Division between the shady side and the less expensive sunny side.

12—Callejón. The passageway between the wooden fence and the grandstand.

13—Asientos de Barrera. Lower and more expensive seats.

14—Asientos de Tendidos. Higher-up seats.

The arena itself is divided into three concentric circles known as los medios (the center), los tercios (the inner ring), and las tablas (the outer ring). Los tercios is indicated by a white chalk line, and the picadors are not allowed to cross it pursuing the bull. The center demarcation line is imaginary, and is used merely to be able to designate that part of the ring when talking or writing about it.

PAGE 32

Only thirty rings hold between 10,-000 and 20,000 "souls," one of which is La Maestranza in Sevilla (top of opposite page). Almost two centuries old, it is the second oldest plaza de toros in Spain and the most beautiful. It is the only ring with sand as golden as represented in the bullfight posters. (Actually it is crushed rock from the mining district of Huelva.) The oldest arena is Ronda's.

The largest plaza in Spain is the Madrid ring (second photograph at left), which seats 23,000 people. But this is dwarfed by the gigantic bowl in Mexico City (shown in the last two photographs), which can cram in over 50,000.

No two rings are exactly alike but most of them follow this basic plan. The best seats are in the sombra or shady half of the ring, and hence are more expensive. A front-row barrera seat for an average corrida will cost approximately ten dollars in Spain, twenty dollars in Mexico, depending upon the matadors who are fighting. Tickets can be obtained through the hotel concerje, at the ticket office in town, or at the bull ring itself just before the fight.

Above, enthusiasts bargain with scalpers in front of a poster which bears the sticker "no tickets"; below, a young ticketless aficionado sneaks his way into the Madrid ring by a perilous route.

PAGE 33

The bullfighters arrive ten or fifteen minutes before the fight begins. Here Manolete talks to admirers in his home town of Córdoba on his way to the back of the ring. (One is the great critic Cossío.)

Usually there are three matadors on the program, but ocasionally there will be four. The most exciting fights are when only two take part. This is called a mano a mano—a "hand-to-hand" contest between two rivals, each matador trying to outdo the other in skill and daring. The first great mano a mano in history was between Costillares and Romero in the eighteenth century. Since then it has been Frascuelo vs. Lagartijo, Espartero vs. Guerra, Machaquito vs. Bombita, Joselito vs. Belmonte, and Manolete vs. Arruza. At the top of the opposite page Joselito (left) and Belmonte (right), whose eight-year rivalry came to be known as "The Golden Age of Bullfighting," line up in front of their cuadrillas waiting tensely for one of their first historic mano a manos to commence.

While they are waiting the toreros either talk briefly among themselves, smoke, pray in the little ring chapel, or avail themselves of the urinal for the meada de miedo—"the big fear leak." One top-flight bullfighter always wore dark costumes because when he heard the opening trumpet he would wet his pants.

"They say Lagartijo used to spit copiously before going in the ring to show his contempt of fear," Juan Belmonte once told me. "But they are liars. We all have mouths as dry as Sahara."

35

36

At exactly the appointed hour the band strikes up. (In Mexico the dramatic "Virgen de la Macarena" and "Cielo Andaluz" are always played before the fight—in Spain there is no one standard song, though "La Morena de Mi Copla" is a favorite. Whatever the title, it is always a pasodoble—a two-step.) The crowd cheers, and the matadors stride out into the arena followed by their banderilleros and the mounted picadors. The drag mules bring up the rear. If there are three matadors, the youngest—that is, the one most recently made a full matador—is in the middle, the next oldest on the left (as you watch them come toward you) and the oldest on the right.[1]

Graduating from novillero to full matador de toros is like going from preliminary boxer to main-eventer; whenever a novillero's manager thinks his fighter has enough public appeal and knows enough to compete with the top-flight matadors a ceremonial fight is arranged where a full matador presents his cape and bull to the newcomer. This is known as "taking the alternative." La alternativa may be taken in another city but it must be "confirmed" in a fight in Madrid. Sometimes novilleros find it more profitable to remain a first-class Matador de Novillos and get all the minor fights they want than to become a Matador de Toros and be crowded off the programs by the big stars. Novilleros are not amateurs; some young newcomers make more than full matadors. They are simply novices who fight younger and smaller animals.

Leading the parade (see frontispiece) are the alguaciles, or constables, dressed in the sixteenth-century costume of Philip the Second's reign. They take no part in the actual fight and simply are there to go through the

[1] If a matador walks with his hat in his hand, it means it is his first fight in that arena. In some plazas it is done when it is the torero's first appearance of the season in that ring.

ceremony of asking the presidente for the key to open the gate which lets in the bulls and to carry out any other orders the presidente might give.

The presidente, usually a town official, sits up in the authorities' box, flanked by one or more ex-bullfighters or experts who advise him. The supreme authority in the ring, he is the one who decides if the bull has had too much punishment from the picadors or if a bull should be returned to the corrals because of a physical defect, or whether or not the matador deserves the ears of the dead animal.

After all the bullfighters have bowed to the presidente, the picadors and the drag mules leave the ring and the matadors and banderilleros sling their ornate dress capes up to friends in the first row to spread out in front of them. The mozos de estoques—the sword boys—hand the toreros their big work capes and then go back to setting up the muletas and preparing the other tools in the passageway (opposite page, photo at right).

PAGE 37 *73*

THE TOOLS

The divisa—ribbons of the bull's stable which are barbed into the withers as the bull enters the ring. This is not done in every plaza.

The capote or capa de brega is used by the matador and his banderilleros. Made of raw silk and rayon they are heavy and stiff enough to be stood up by themselves. Magenta on the outside, they are yellow on the inside.

The picador's lance, called the pica (8 feet long).

The banderillas (26 inches long).

Notched stick is inserted and fixed to the cloth with a screweye to give the matador a handle.

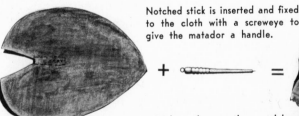

Muleta, the way the sword boy hands it to his matador.

Muleta spread out flat.

The puntilla, or coup de grâce dagger.

The sword, or estoque. Blade is bent at the end so that it will curve down to the aorta.

The descabello sword, used only after entering to kill at least once with the regular estoque.

The arena is cleared, the kettledrum rumbles, a trumpet blares, the crowd hushes expectantly, and the toril gate is jerked open.

Into the ring explodes the first bull of the afternoon. Although nothing has been done to make him angry, he charges into the arena knowing what he is there for and immediately starts looking for something to kill. He gallops at an amazing speed around the empty circle, perhaps stopping to lower his great head and hook tentatively into the barrera—the heavy board fence—as the bull below is about to do.

The senior matador—who is required to fight the first and fourth bulls—stands behind the barrera watching every move and characteristic of the animal intently. Then he will turn to a banderillero, as Dominguín is doing, at the right, and nod.

"Run him," he might order. "Double this creature for me."

This is the first minute of an encounter which will last approximately twenty minutes.

ACT I
THE DOUBLING

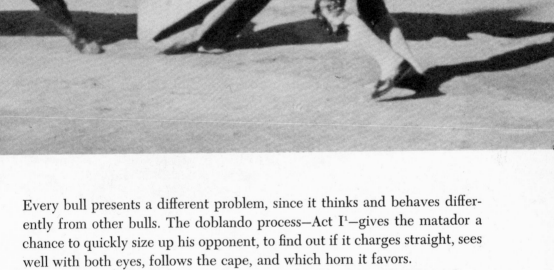

Every bull presents a different problem, since it thinks and behaves differently from other bulls. The doblando process—Act I[1]—gives the matador a chance to quickly size up his opponent, to find out if it charges straight, sees well with both eyes, follows the cape, and which horn it favors.

The banderillero should do this initial caping with one hand. With no attempt at style, he approaches the animal cautiously and flings out the cape in front of him, holding on to one end. The animal charges the cape, not because of its color (bulls are color-blind) but because of its motion. The banderillero drags the cape in front of the bull's nose, stepping back out of the way of danger as he does. He turns as the bull wheels, and repeats the performance once or twice more before jumping over the fence or sliding through one of the burladero openings.

This brief caping is done only as a prelude to the matador's work, and the performance of the banderillero is intended to be functional, not graceful or daring. If there is applause at this time it is usually meant for the

[1] Most writings refer to "the three tercios" (thirds) of the corrida: the act of the picadors, the act of the banderillas, and the act of the death. But actually modern bullfighting has been refined to seven acts.

breeder of the bull for having sent a courageous, hard-charging animal into the arena.

The doubling is an important part of the fight from the matador's standpoint, but it is neither artistic nor very dangerous, since the banderillero, unlike the matador, can crouch over safely, jitter his feet out of the way of the bull, and stay yards away from the deadly horns. He can even throw down his cape and dive over the fence if he finds himself in a dangerous spot, an act which would disgrace the matador.

However, mayhem is possible to everyone in the arena from the first moment the bull enters it. In the photograph above, the banderillero Maera made a false move while doing his routine job of doubling a bull and the animal lost no time in lacing a horn in and out of the man's left leg, a painful way of showing his matador which horn the bull favored.

ACT II
THE MATADOR'S FIRST CAPEWORK

A great expectancy hangs over the crowd now, for the matador must make his appearance and cape the bull.

This is designed to slow the bull down before the picadors, but more important, it gives the matador a chance to show the capework that he has practiced years to perfect.

In olden times the point of bullfighting was simply to get in the ring with a bull, dodge out of the way of its charges, wear it down, and kill it. The entire emphasis was on the kill. Modern bullfighting, however, places the importance on the grace and skill with which a matador handles the cape and muleta. Simply dodging out of the way of a bull while flinging a cape in its face the way the banderillero did in the doubling does not exhibit grace or skill or courage, which are what the crowd has come to see; they have paid money to see men behave the opposite of the way *they* would act if confronted with a charging bull.

The standard *lance* or *pase* for the matador to do at this time in the fight is la verónica. (It is named after the woman who is said to have held out a cloth to Christ on the road to Calvary much as a cape is held.)

The verónica is the basic pass of bullfighting. It is at once the simplest yet the most difficult pass. It can be made the most dangerous and sublime, if the matador wants to stand straight and languidly let the near horn graze by two inches from his thighs; or it can be made ludicrously safe if he chooses to crouch over and jerkily pass the bull two yards from his body.[1]

The crowd watches eagerly as the matador bites the collar of the cape and holds it by his teeth while he slides his hands down the cloth for the proper grip. Then he slips through the burladero opening in the fence and strides out in front of the bull, chanting gutturally, "Toro, ah-ha-ha-ha!" to

[1] Sidney Franklin, the only American to become a full matador, once told me that the greatest series of verónicas he ever saw executed was done by Charlie Chaplin in a session of "toreo de salón"—fooling around with a cape in a living room. Chaplin had seen several good toreros perform, and with his imitative genius he was able not only to duplicate but to improve upon a maneuver which takes years to master.

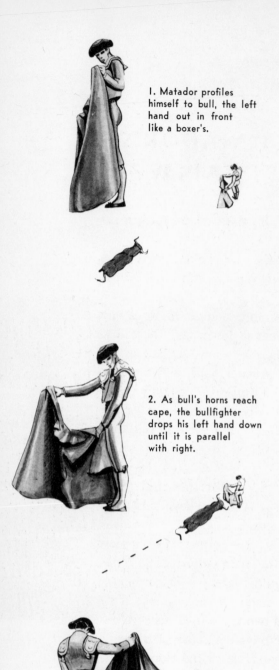

1. Matador profiles himself to bull, the left hand out in front like a boxer's.

2. As bull's horns reach cape, the bullfighter drops his left hand down until it is parallel with right.

3. Right hand and left hand swing cape through to take bull by.

attract its attention away from where the banderillero has gone through or over the barrera.

THE VERONICA

The bullfighter usually takes the bull wide on the first pass on each side to further observe how it handles its head and to let it get the first erratic jumps and bucks out of it. At the right the great, coldly perfect Mexican Armillita takes an unusually marked bull by on the first verónica. Notice how straight and relaxed he is; the easier a pass looks the harder it is to do, and the better it is being done.

The bull wheels at the end of the pass and again charges the tantalizing cloth. The middle bull is probably cowardly since it prefers to jump out with its hoofs instead of burying its head in the cape.

The most important single thing for the beginning aficionado to concentrate on is the matador's feet. He may keep them together or far apart, like Antonio Ordóñez in the bottom picture, but once he has planted his feet and taken his stand he should not step back as the bull charges until the horns are past his legs. Ordóñez, a top young Spanish matador, is the son of Niño de la Palma, who reputedly was the proto-

type of the young torero in *The Sun Also Rises,* as well as the old banderillero in *Matador.* In this photo he is illustrating the difficult-to-explain expression "cargando la suerte," which is a sort of following through of a pass with the upper body.

45

46

"Parar, mandar, y templar" are the three rules for good capework, either with the capote or the muleta. Knowing what they mean will explain to a person seeing his first corrida why the thousands of people in the audience roar "Olé!" (supposedly derived from the Moors' cry of "Allah") for one pass and remain in sullen and abused silence after another that to the neophyte looks exactly the same. The man swung the cape, didn't he, and the bull charged by and missed him, didn't it? What was the difference between that pass and the other one?

Perhaps the matador parar-ed but didn't mandar and templar. Of the three requisites mandar is the most important. It means controlling the bull, making him follow the cape wherever and however the man wants him to go. It takes experience and nerve. Parar takes merely nerve. Parar means planting one's feet on the ground as the bull charges and not sliding them back, no matter how close the horn slices by. Templar always comes after the other ingredients and is harder to define. Impossible to capture in a photo, it is a slowing down, a prolongation of the danger of the bull's charge, an insouciance and grace in the man's movements which mean the difference between a willing courageous hacker like Martorell and a great artist like Domingo Ortega, or Pepe Luis Vásquez. Even a person seeing his first fight will recognize true *temple* if he is lucky enough to see it.

PAGE 46

As Hemingway says, in what is still the finest philosophical approach to bullfighting written in English: "The fact is that the gypsy, Cagancho, can sometimes, through the marvellous wrists that he has, perform the usual movements of bullfighting so slowly they become, to old-time bullfighting, as the slow motion picture is to the ordinary motion picture. It is as though a diver could control his speed in the air and prolong the vision of a swan dive, which is a jerk in actual life, although in photographs it seems a long glide, to make it a long glide like the dives and leaps we sometimes take in dreams."

At left below, El Soldado is mandando—gaining control—staying on top of the bull as he executes his verónica, crowding it, forcing it to stay with the cape and do his bidding. The uninitiate often protests: "But this looks easy—the animal always goes at the cape!" It goes at the cape and not the man only because the man's skill and knowledge of bulls *make* it go at the cape. And if it looks easy you are watching experts.

With every verónica the man should be working closer to the bull. Here Pascual Márquez stands straight and moves only his arms as fourteen hundred pounds of infuriated animal hurtle past him. (Fighting bulls are usually black, and bulls like this are not common. A list of terms for the different variations of colorings can be found at the end of the book.)

PAGE 47

49

Just how close the bull is permitted to come to the man is shown graphically in this photograph of the great Belmonte. To gauge the angle of the bull's charge so exactly that the horn rubs against his stomach as it goes by and at the same time execute a beautiful, rhythmic figure with the cape, a man must be an artist. A bullfighter is a dancer, but a dancer on a tightrope. The passes he does are as formalized and laboriously practiced as the *entrechat* and *tour jeté*, but whereas if the ballet dancer makes a

mistake on the stage he merely loses face, the matador can lose a leg or his life. Belmonte worked so close to the animals and was tossed so often that he was known as "the torero of four olés and an ay!"

It is unusual to attend two or three fights without seeing at least one person tossed. It comes usually with no warning. Perhaps the matador is working closer and closer to his adversary's horns, when a slight unpredictable shake of the animal's head sends him flying into the air.

Before the bull can gore the man on the ground, his banderilleros or the other matadors rush to his assistance, by flashing capes in the bull's face. The man buries his head in his hands and remains as still as possible, hoping the animal will leave his inanimate form for the swirl and movement of the capotes. Above, Dominguín and Andaluz run to aid Litri.

When the bull is lured to another part of the ring, the injured man is gathered up and rushed out of the arena, and down the passageway to the ring infirmary.

In the last few years the illegal practice of doctoring the bulls' horns has become prevalent in Spain in order to minimize the danger of horn wounds. It consists of putting a bull in a squeeze chute, taking off an inch or so of horn, and then refiling the end to a not-so-sharp point. Besides lessening the chances of the horns penetrating, it also upsets the bull's ability to judge his thrusts accurately, since he is used to fighting with longer weapons. The top bullfighters instituted this ruinous innovation by saying, "We won't use your bulls unless they're 'shaved,'" and now nearly all the bull breeders have had to give in to them. The strange thing is that there seem to be almost as many horn wounds as before, and an ironic fact which has never been published before is that Camará, Manolete's manager, saw to it that the bulls of his matador's last fight had their horns "afeitados." Nevertheless, Islero managed to get fifteen inches of his blunted splintery right horn into the man's body. Recent public protest is causing "shaving" to disappear.

Horn wounds are dirty because the bull's horns are dirty, and the doctor's principal problem is preventing infection. Penicillin has reduced the mortality rate considerably.

"If I am to get it," the bullfighter prays, "let it be in Madrid," for the great specialists in horn wounds are in Madrid. The best of them all, Jiménez Guinea, was rushed to Linares in southern Spain after Manolete was gored, but the wound was too terrible, and the doctor could only watch him die. Like the majority of cornadas it was a groin wound. The upper legs and crotch are the most common places for injuries. Toreros wear no protection under the silk and gold costume, not even an athletic supporter. If the matador is so badly injured that he cannot continue the fight, his bull automatically goes to the next matador, who must kill this bull as well as his own two.

PAGE 51

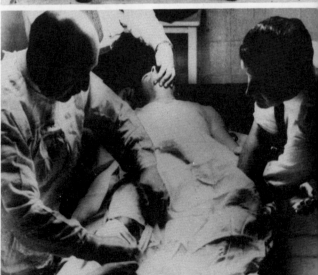

55

But assuming that the matador is not injured in the first passes, after he has done several good verónicas, perhaps four or five, he must end the series elegantly. The usual way of finishing off a set of verónicas is with a half-verónica.

The media-verónica starts like a regular verónica except that halfway through the pass the matador gathers up the cape on his hip, as in the picture above. Following the tight swirl of the cloth wrenches the bull

56

around in less than its own length, and since it has charged hard many times without hitting anything solid, it is usually glad to stop for a breather. The matador takes the cape off his hip with one hand (below, left) and stalks away into the roar of the crowd, reasonably sure that the bull will not attack when he turns his back to walk to the fence.

57

A variation of the media-verónica is this one done on one knee by the great Mexican Lorenzo Garza. A kneeling pass is automatically more dangerous because it is harder for the matador to get out of the bull's way if it should suddenly charge toward him instead of the cape; also there is more chance of a chest or head wound. However, many purists claim that kneeling in a bull ring is an acrobatic trick rather than classic toreo.

A flamboyant way of ending a series of verónicas is with the rebolera. Again, the pass is begun like a verónica, but as the bull's horns go by the man's body, he lets go of the cape with one hand and snaps the cloth around his waist with the other, making it blossom out around his body like a dancer's skirt. When done correctly the way Ricardo Torres and the gypsy Cagancho are doing in the first two photos, it can be a very beautiful and moving thing. Unfortunately one too often sees the matador do the rebolera a yard or more from the animal, as in the third photo, in which case, though a pretty little maneuver, it is as meaningless as though he were doing it in the safety of his living room.

Coming under the heading of unscheduled events are two things that can occur at this point to interrupt the proceedings. The first is an espontáneo—a spontaneous one.

Though becoming a bullfighter is the aspiration of every young Spaniard, since it is virtually the only way for a poor boy to attain wealth and fame, there is little opportunity for the hopefuls to break into the game. Most bullfighters come from bullfighting fathers or have relations connected with bullfighting who can secure them invitations to tientas, where the boys practice and eventually come to the attention of some

PAGE 54

manager or promoter who bills them for a second-rate novillada. There are
a few haphazard schools of tauromachy (lower left) but they cost money -
and they have never turned out a first-class torero. The aspirant without a
patron must get his practice by wangling his way to tientas or by furtive and
illegal caping of bulls in the fields. To get the opportunity to show his skill
to a manager or promoter is very difficult, and many boys must resort to
being espontáneos. This consists of gulping several belts of cognac for
courage, smuggling a tattered muleta cape and stick for a sword under one's
"americana" jacket, and going to a regular corrida de toros or a novillada.
He waits until the matador has finished a series of passes and has walked
away from the bull to the fence. Then, working his furtive way down from
a cheap seat, he pulls out his muleta and leaps into the arena. He capes the
bull as fancily as he can and the crowd loves it, especially if he shows any
talent, as this boy above does. The professional bullfighters, however, don't
want him messing up the ritual, and they try to get the bull away as quickly
as possible. If the espontáneo isn't gored or slammed out of the ring, like the

PAGE 55

luckless fellow above, left, the police and the bullfighters hustle him out of the ring. He will probably have to do some time in jail for his exploit, but it's possible that when he gets out, if he showed some graceful passes, a manager or impresario will give him a chance in some small ring.

Another unscheduled event is the abrupt exit of the adversary. If a bull is going to jump out of the ring he often does it at this juncture of the fight. Sometimes a bull leaps the fence in pursuit of a man, but jumping out generally indicates that the bull is manso—cowardly—and that he is trying to get back to the safety of the corrals. Notice how easily the bulls are clearing the high fence. Once the bull is in the callejón—or passageway—great confusion ensues, to the delight of the crowd sitting safely in the stands. Here six picadors, their right legs encased in thirty pounds of armor, spill into the

66
6:

ring clumsily to get away from the lethal horns. Finally a gate into the ring is opened which blocks off the passageway and the bull returns to the ring. The bull immediately drives at the men in the ring and the diving-over-the-fence process is repeated in reverse.

In the photo below the bull has managed to get up into the stands of the Málaga ring, fortunately a most unusual occurrence. The fans, who moments before were upbraiding the bullfighters for not working closer, have suddenly developed a healthier respect for the animal. Luckily the bullfighting Dominguín brothers were in the audience, and can be seen behind the bull, rushing to the rescue. With their coats they managed to cape the bull out an exit, down the stairs, and into the ring without anyone getting hurt.

PAGE 59

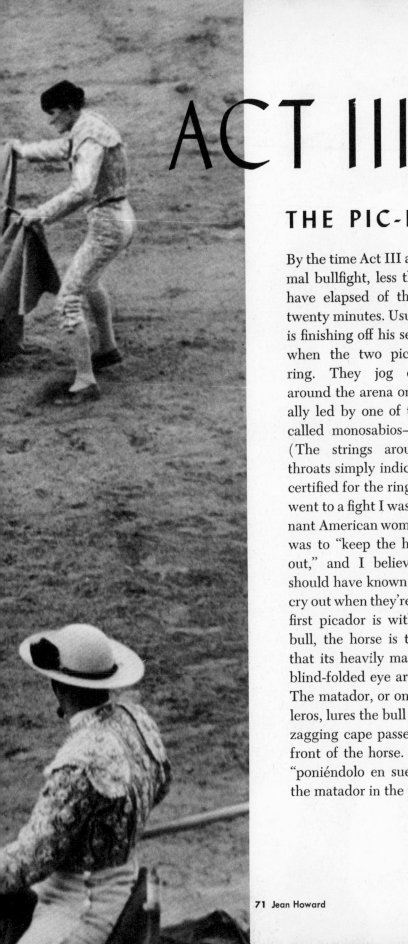

ACT III

THE PIC-ING

By the time Act III arrives in the normal bullfight, less than five minutes have elapsed of the approximately twenty minutes. Usually the matador is finishing off his series of verónicas when the two picadors enter the ring. They jog counterclockwise around the arena on their nags, usually led by one of the ring servants called monosabios—"wise-monkeys." (The strings around the horses' throats simply indicate that they are certified for the ring. The first time I went to a fight I was told by an indignant American woman that the string was to "keep the horse from crying out," and I believed it, though I should have known that horses don't cry out when they're hurt.) When the first picador is within range of the bull, the horse is turned around so that its heavily mattressed side and blind-folded eye are facing the bull. The matador, or one of his banderilleros, lures the bull by a series of zigzagging cape passes into position in front of the horse. This is known as "poniéndolo en suerte." Notice that the matador in the photo is not striv-

PAGE 61

ing for any stiff-kneed elegance or planting of the feet, since this is merely a functional procedure and the audience is not looking for cape styling at this juncture of the fight. (The torero is Rovira, Argentina's pride.)

When the bull spots the horse he breaks into a hard charge. The picador shoots his lance into the bull's withers as the horns hit the mattress-protected flank of his mount, and sliding his hand down the eight-foot pole where he can grip it securely, he puts his full weight on the bull.

No one—except Hemingway's little Old Lady—derives pleasure from watching this act, but it is necessary. The purpose of the picador is, first, to weaken the bull's powerful neck muscles so that the animal will be right for the muleta passes and kill to follow. Secondly, it is important to give the bull encouragement by letting it hit the mattressed horse after having charged so many times at the capes and hit nothing.

If the bull has any power the horse and rider go down on the first charge.

I saw a grim double-header once in Málaga: the picador was slammed up against the barrera so hard that his back was snapped like a saltine, and a woman seeing it from the first row of the stands had a heart attack, dying before the picador did.

The padded horse is usually not hurt in the tossing, but he and the picador are immediately in trouble. Five examples of the predicaments picadors can get into are shown on these pages. With his heavy, armored leg, a fallen picador is helpless, and must depend upon the torero's cape for rescue.

74, 75

76, 77

ACT IV THE QUITES

The verb quitar in Spanish means to "take away from," and *un quite* (oon kee'-tay) means taking the bull away from the horse or rescuing a fallen picador or torero. After each of the three charges a bull is required to make at the picador, the animal must be lured away by the three matadors in turn. Each tries to outdo the other in the gracefulness and risk-taking of the passes, and this is often the most competitive and exciting part of the fight. It is in the *quites* that a matador can show the variety of his capework. Sometimes the matador stays with the basic verónica as Manolo González is doing here with this beautiful bull, but usually the more complicated passes are chosen.

One of the commonest (and prettiest) is the chicuelina pass, invented by Chicuelo. The matador comes up behind the bull as it is slamming the horse around or, as in the case of the preceding photos, attacking the fallen picador. Flashing his cape in the animal's face, he shouts: "Toro—ah-ha-ha!" The bull swerves away from his victim to drive at the annoying voice and cape, and the bullfighter runs backward to lure the animal away from the area. Once he has the bull far enough away so that there is no danger that it will recharge the picador unexpectedly, the matador stops his running tactics. He "cites" the bull, holding the cape as though for the verónica.

PAGE 66

78

When the bull's horn is just going by the man's legs, he tucks his right arm into his body, spins in toward the bull, and revolves completely around, ready to repeat the maneuver for the next charge.

Here is the chicuelina as performed by Manolo Bienvenida (in the two top pictures) and its inventor, Chicuelo. It is a purely ornamental pass; control is sacrificed when the cape is snatched from the face of the animal, the man taking advantage of the animal's momentum. As in all maneuvers made in the ring,

79, 80
81

the slower it is executed, the more casually the man prolongs the danger to himself, the more moving the pass is to watch.

After three or more chicuelinas, depending upon how well the bull is charging, the matador finishes off the series with a media-verónica or a rebolera. At top left the matador lets go of the cape with his left hand for the first stage of the rebolera and then he swirls the cape around his waist, the right hand passing the cape to his left again behind his back.

In the photo below, Manolo González tangled in his cape while executing a rebolera and was sent to the hospital for a month.

82, 83

It is no disgrace to be tossed. It does imply a lack of control over the bull, but it also indicates that the man was working close to the animal and was not playing it safe. The gored matador will find he has lost no popularity when he is released from the hospital. What he must worry about is whether or not he has lost his nerve. It is hard to go back to confronting a pair of horns when the clammy feel of the doctor's rubber gloves is still on one's flesh, and many a brilliant young star has been eclipsed by a bad wound. Whenever a new "fenómeno" is touted to the skies the café experts will say, "Yes, but let us wait until he has his baptism of blood." The first bad wound is the crucial one; Spaniards say a man sheds his brave blood first, then comes "fear of the hule"—the operating table's oilcloth sheet.

THE SECOND PIC-ING

After the first *quite* is finished, the bull is again maneuvered into position in front of one of the picadors. Although the bull has received the lance thrust a few inches into the flesh of his withers, he is encouraged by having tossed the first horse and charges fiercely. Here the bull has charged so hard and eagerly that it has dug its horns into the sand and flipped itself end over end; a brave bull holds his head very low when he charges while a cowardly bull keeps his high.

"I like everything but the horses" is the most common statement by Americans about la fiesta brava. Then someone else always adds: "Well, they're only glue-factory nags anyway" (as though purebred horses felt pain more keenly than their less aristocratic brethren!).

PAGE 69

"The victims of the fiesta," as Spaniards refer to the horses, are indeed pathetic creatures, and no one enjoys seeing them slammed around; but it is necessary that the bull hit something solid for encouragement and that his neck muscles be weakened if the fight is to continue as prescribed. The horses have been protected by the heavy peto mattress for twenty-five years, and it is not often one sees a horse killed in the arena these days. Perhaps the outright death of olden times was preferable to the repeated onslaughts the horses are exposed to now. It's been said that bullfighting is "indefensible but irresistible"; the act of the pic-ing is surely its most resistible component.

But hear Mr. Hemingway on the subject of people and the horses: "If they sincerely identify themselves with animals they will suffer terribly, more so perhaps than the horse; since a man who has been wounded knows that the pain of a wound does not commence until about half an hour after it has been received and there is no proportional relation in pain to the horrible aspect of the wound; the pain of an abdominal wound does not come at the time but later with the gas pains and the beginning of peritonitis; a pulled ligament or a broken bone, though, hurts at once and terribly; but these things

PAGE 70

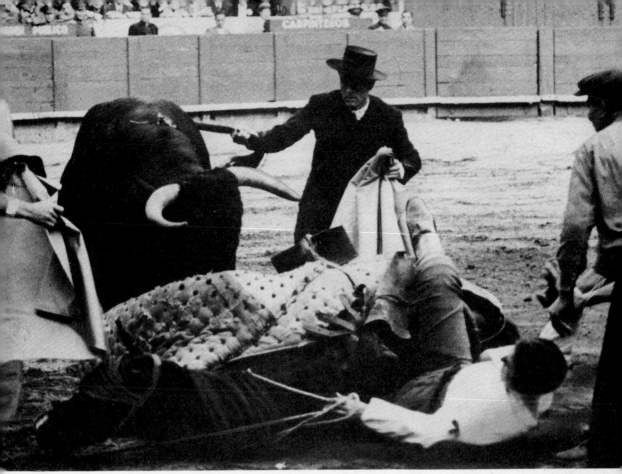

are not known or they are ignored by the person who has identified himself with the animal and he will suffer genuinely and terribly, seeing only this aspect of the bullfight, while, when a horse pulls up lame in a steeplechase, he will not suffer at all and consider it merely regrettable."

At left the bull lifts horse and rider up as Manolo González rushes to the *quite*. A famous painting, "An Opportune *Quite*," depicts Christ saving a fallen torero with his robe this way.

Sometimes a bull refuses to leave the inviting bulk of the fallen picador for a mere cape, and the matador must slap or kick the bull's stern or yank its tail to lure it away as in the photograph above. The matador is dressed in "traje corto" instead of a suit of lights, because it is *un festival*. The mono-sabio at the right is rushing to the picador's aid.

"Wise-monkeys"—so named after a similarly dressed troupe of trained monkeys of the 1850's—have saved countless toreros' lives. Simón, the Mexican, is a famous heroic monosabio.

PAGE 71

THE SECOND QUITE

The second *quite* is performed by the matador second in respect to seniority. He should try to outdo the first *quite* and garner more applause.

In the top left photograph the Mexican, Garza—"Lorenzo el Magnífico"—chooses a gaonera pass, invented by the great Mexican fighter, Rodolfo Gaona. Starting as in a verónica, the bullfighter regally flips the cape over his head as soon as the horn passes his legs. Holding the cape in back of his body, his legs completely exposed, the man makes the bull charge back and forth in front of him. The pass is a verónica

88, 89

90

in theory, but with the dangerous difference that the cape is not a shield in front of the body. Again the points to watch are the lack of movement by the feet, the proximity of the man to the animal, and the slowness of the man's arm movements.

Vicente Barrera (top, right) is letting the horn come so close that he must rise up on tiptoe and arch his body to escape a goring by inches. In the center photograph, Jesús Córdoba lets the horn brush past his chest, while, below, Carlos Arruza, a master of the varied *quite*, calmly watches the horn graze by his legs.

PAGE 73

91, 92

93

94

A series of gaoneras is generally ended with a rebolera or a serpentina.
Above, the serpentina starts with a spectacular flourish—
and then is pulled around the waist in the manner of the rebolera—
PAGE 74

95

and the bullfighter strides off arrogantly, disdain on his face.

"How can a man just turn his back on the bull and walk away?" people ask incredulously when they see it for the first time. The bullfighter only does it when the bull has charged hard several times, is winded, and has been "fixed" by a sudden wrenching pass. An experienced torero knows enough about bulls to know when he can get away with it. If he doesn't know his bull psychology well enough, this is what can happen.

PAGE 75

THE THIRD PIC-ING

99

Actually, the regulations decree that a bull must take four varas, but custom—because of the decreasing size of the modern bull and the horse's protective mattress—have reduced the number to three. Often the matador will earn the applause of the crowd by doffing his montera to the presidente and requesting that the suerte (the act) be changed after the bull has taken only two pics. I have seen Arruza order the picadors out of the ring without a single vara, because of the smallness of the bulls.

A bull should be pic-ed just behind the hump of tossing muscle, neither too far forward nor too far back. This bull is being pic-ed well except that the puya (the point) has been placed a little off center.

The picador should keep his horse more or less at right angles to the bull while pic-ing, giving the bull the opportunity to pull away at any time to go at the man making the *quite*. Turning the horse's head in toward the bull after the pic is placed, thereby blocking its natural exit and subjecting it to more grinding by the picador, is called "doing the carioca." It is highly illegal and very common, unfortunately.

On the preceding page, the picador has pic-ed too far back and too deep in an illegal manner that can cripple the bull and ruin the fight. The tope—the little circular shield intended to prevent the lance from going in beyond the puya point—has been sunk out of sight in the bull's neck.

Lamentably, one has come to expect every job of pic-ing to be as bad or worse than this. The crowd will howl, the picador will be fined, but the criminal practice will go on until the authorities change the archaic design of the puya so that it cannot penetrate too deeply. Simply enlarging the tope shield would take care of most of the abuses, and that step is being considered.

PAGE 78

THE THIRD QUITE

The third "sword" takes the bull away from the horse, as he is doing in the photograph on page 76, and immediately sets about trying to outdo the other two matadors.

One of the flashiest passes with the cape is the farol, where the matador flips the cape over his head while at the same time spinning in toward the animal. It is automatically a dangerous pass since the man loses sight of his adversary's head while executing it. Getting down on one's knees while doing it makes it much more dangerous, as there's no stepping out of the way at the last minute. Below, Arruza seems certain to get his head spiked on a horn, but his timing and judgment are so superb that the weapon merely grazed his face as thousands of people screamed with delighted horror. Again, at the top of the next page, Arruza seems headed for a goring as he does a frighteningly close farol de rodillas. Actually, with only five almost-fatal horn wounds, thirty-three-year-old Arruza is one of the least punished of the top bullfighters in spite of the incredible chances he continues to take after twenty-one years of fighting. ("Sure, I'm afraid," he said to me once, "but hunger wounds worse than the bulls.")

PAGE 79

An impression of the surprising speed of a fighting bull is shown in the photo at the lower left of Luis Miguel Dominguín doing a farol de rodillas.

A specialty of Dominguín's is the larga cambiada. This can be used as the first part of a *quite* series, but Dominguín often does it at the very beginning of the fight as he is in the picture above. Getting on his knees in front of the toril gate he flings his cape out in front of him, holding on to one end with his right hand. As the bull bursts out into the sunlight and bears down on him he swirls the cape over his left shoulder and the bull veers after it. It is a beautiful and dangerous pass, dangerous since the course of the bull which is charging for the left side of the man must be changed to make him pass on the right. The novillero Márquez tried this pass, at the right, and only succeeded in making the bull change his course half way.[1]

104

[1] I only tried doing a larga cambiada once. It was at a festival and I was called down from the stands to fight unexpectedly. I was full of manzanilla or I wouldn't have tried it in the first place, but I did, and like Márquez I succeeded in changing the bull's course only halfway over. The left horn struck me in the chest with tremendous force, but it was one of those believe-it-or-not items. A few minutes before, a girl had asked me to keep her gold cigarette case for her and had slipped it into my breast pocket. When she got it back it was very dented.

PAGE 81

There are many more types of passes used for the *quites*. Below is el galleo created by the immortal Joselito el Gallo and rarely seen since his death in 1920. It consisted of placing the capote over the shoulders as though it were a cloak and running leisurely in front of the hooking bull.

Another beautiful *quite* which one seldom sees these days is the mariposa—the butterfly pass—at the upper right. Invented by Marcial Lalanda, the cape is held behind the back as though for a gaonera, but unlike that pass, the man walks backward slowly crisscrossing the bull in front of his body as it charges at alternate halves of the cape.

The Mexicans give more importance to variety in the *quites* than do the Spaniards, and they have several passes that are not seen in Hispanic repertoires. At the lower right Arruza does a hair-raising reverse version of a chicuelina. Notice appropriate ambulance ad in background!

PAGE 82

ACT V

THE BANDERILLAS

Approximately ten or twelve minutes of the fight have gone by when the trumpet sounds for the picadors to retire from the ring. It is time for the banderillas to be placed.

If the torero is not one of the matadors who place their own banderillas, he withdraws to the fence and studies the bull as Belmonte is doing here. One of the matador's banderilleros takes a pair of the colored, paper-frilled, barbed sticks, and, after spitting on his fingers and moistening the points (for luck, and to make them slip in easier) he runs into the arena.

The most common of the half-dozen ways of putting in banderillas is al cuarteo, quartering the circle. This maneuver is based on the principle that the man can turn in less area than the bull, since he has only two legs to the bull's four. This diagram and the photos on the next page show how a banderillero cites the animal from a stationary position, then breaks off to the side when the bull starts his charge. By running in a tight arc he cuts inside the bull's horns, places the banderillas, and lets momentum carry the bull beyond striking distance. The prick of the barbs usually distracts the bull and keeps it from pursuing the man, who heads for the fence.

The point of banderillas is debatable. Theoretically they are to tire the neck muscles more and also to correct any hooking mannerism by placing them on the opposite side of the hook. Experts disagree on the unimportance or importance of "los palitroques," however.

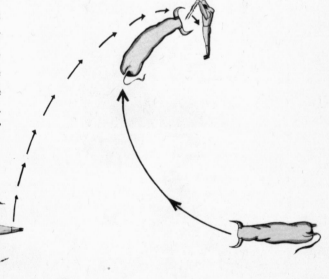

Beginning aficionados usually prefer the banderillas to all else in the ring, because it seems miraculous to them that a virtually unarmed man can get so close to the bull and come out unscathed. However, the average placing of the banderillas by the banderilleros is a safe affair; it is not a dangerous feat simply to place a pair of sticks while avoiding a bull's charge the way the banderilleros at the right are doing. These men are competent hacks doing their unartistic routine job. But turn the page!

PAGE 86

109

Like everything else in the ring, it can be made as beautiful and dangerous as a man's skill and courage permits. If the matador himself places the banderillas, one is apt to see a beautiful athletic exhibition. The three things to watch in banderillas are: how straight a man's body is as he places the sticks, how close he is to the bull's horns, and how high he raises his arms.

Here are four superb examples of how exciting the placing of banderillas can be.

Contrast the uninspired, safe drabness of the banderillero in the photograph at the top of the preceding page with the statuesqueness of Pepe Dominguín at left, above, the proximity of Carlos Arruza to the bull below, and his almost airborne grace in the pictures on the opposite page.

Arruza, a Mexican, is a matador, but also the world's greatest banderillero. The Mexicans give more importance to the banderillas than do the Spaniards and hence they have always been better at it. Most Mexican matadors know how to place their own sticks, while most Spanish matadors do not.

PAGE 88

112
113

114
115

1. Man "cites" bull by shouting and giving a little spring into the air.

2. Man waits until horns almost reach his legs. Suddenly he jumps, leg out to the side, swinging his body as though he were going in that direction. Bull swerves to intercept him.

3. Bullfighter sucks back leg at last moment, pivots, and drives the barbed sticks into the bull's withers.

A more spectacular and rarer way of placing the banderillas is al quiebro, demonstrated above. In the photo below, Morenito de Talavera starts to "break" the bull's charge to one side by feinting out with his leg.

On the opposite page, Arruza has just drawn back his leg and is placing the sticks perfectly while letting the horn skim by his chest. Below that, Carnicerito places them with his back up against the fence dangerously.

PAGE 90

121

In the upper picture opposite, Niño de la Palma demonstrates how to let a horn scrape one's ribcage while placing a pair of "los garapullos."

At right is a trick which is seldom seen, and that is just as well since it belongs more in a circus than a bull ring. The man will rise from the chair at the last minute, make the bull swerve in the manner of the al quiebro maneuver, and place the banderillas. It is unaesthetic. It is dangerous, yes; but then so is driving while drinking, and that's no fun to watch.

Al quiebro comes from the verb quebrar—to break—and the difficulty in placing the sticks in this manner is in judging the animal's speed and knowing exactly when to break the line of its charge. If the swerving is done too soon the bull will be tricked off its course but then will have time to become unfooled and hook into the man.

If it is done too late—well, below, opposite, is a ludicrously pathetic reminder of why it is not good to quebrar too late. Though the boy looks carefree enough with fifteen inches of horn in his body, this wound was classified as "gravísimo," and he almost died.

A highly detailed medical report of a cornada suffered during a fight appears the next day in the newspapers, and the doctors will classify the wound "prognóstico reservado" or "leve" if it is not serious. The progression follows: grave, muy grave, and gravísimo. After that it's "muerto."

PAGE 93

ACT VI THE FAENA

When the last pair of banderillas is placed (sometimes only two pairs if the presidente thinks the bull seems overly tired) a trumpet signals for the final phase of the fight—la faena de muleta, literally, the muleta task.

The beginning aficionado likes the different suertes in this order: banderillas, capework, and lastly the muleta work. The expert likes them in the reverse order. The modern matador stands or falls on his reputation as a muletero. He may swing a capote like Gitanillo de Triana, place banderillas like Maera, and kill like Fuentes Bejarano, but if he does not have a feeling for the small red flannel rag he will never rise to the top.

While not as obviously flashy as the swirling cape of the first part of the fight, the muleta work is more dangerous and can be much more moving after the beginner learns what to look for. It is more dangerous because it presents half the target to the bull that the cape does, and most of the passes leave the man's body exposed, giving the bull his choice of the small cloth or the inviting bulk of the matador's legs.

The sword boy passes the folded muleta over the fence to his matador, who takes it in his left hand and then clamps the sword to it with his thumb. (A wooden sword is often substituted for the steel one because of weight and maneuverability.) With the montera hat in his right hand the matador makes the formal routine request of the presidente to kill the bull, as Manolete is doing here. He will then sometimes rededicate the bull to someone in the audience, either a personal friend or some prominent figure, saying something like: "Va por ti—vamos a ver lo que se puede hacer con este bravísimo toro." ("It goes for you—let us see what can be done with this very brave bull.") The honored person must reciprocate later with a fine present.

He then wheels and tosses his montera back over his shoulder up into the stands to the honored person. Often the matador dedicates the bull to the crowd by holding up his montera and pivoting slowly to include the whole ring. When a bullfighter does this you can be sure that he knows he has a good bull and intends to put up the best faena he can with it. After the brindis—the dedication—the matador shakes out the muleta and spreads it

PAGE 95

123

with the sword. (The muleta is frequently described as "heart-shaped" by magazine writers who decide to invade the literary bull ring; that is a true description of the cloth's basic shape, but not the way it looks when it is seen in the arena. See page 37).

The bull has now been caped by the peones into the section of the ring where the matador wants to fight him, since bulls act differently in different areas of the ring. Sometimes the animal takes over a certain part of the ring for his own which is known as his querencia, and he will try to return there whenever allowed. If he has cowardly tendencies his main querencia will be near the toril gate, where he first came into the ring, since he knows it leads back to the safety of the corral and the other bulls. He might also have secondary querencias where he feels he gained a victory by slamming a horse or a man around. A bull in his querencia, as in the photo above, fights a dangerous, counter-punching, come-in-and-get-me type of fight. Because it is impossible for a matador to do beautiful passes with an animal which won't charge hard and freely, the bull is lured to another part of the ring.

This business of querencias and terrains is a complicated subject, puzzling to beginners, and very difficult to explain. Bullfighters are the worst at explaining it, for when they are stalking a bull they don't think in terms of "the man's terrain" and "the bull's terrain," but only "If I take him here I can get away with it," or "I'd better not try to take him there or he'll veer into me."

This knowledge comes from observing or fighting hundreds of bulls. The experienced aficionado in the audience recognizes it when a bullfighter fights the bull in a difficult terrain and appreciates it. For example, since bulls tend to swerve away from the fence when they charge, a primary rule is to keep one's back to the boards when fighting in the inner third of the arena so that the bull will veer ringward and not into one's legs. Therefore, when a man passes the bull in between him and the fence, most of the aficionados know he is doing a dangerous thing. (And just to complicate things, one out of about every 100 bulls has a tendency to swerve *into* the fence and, therefore, it is safer with that particular bull to pass him while facing the boards!)

Different bulls take querencias with varying degrees of affection. While going away from their main querencia, some will charge reluctantly and perhaps put on the brakes halfway through the pass, to the great danger to the man. On the return pass, the animal will charge beautifully and straight—because it is heading toward its querencia. The man can then stand very close to the horn as it goes by and impress some of the crowd, but the experts will know that the bull is just heading home to its querencia, paying little attention to the torero, and that the man is simply "taking advantage of the trip." Juan Belmonte's "revolution" of tauromachy stemmed from his fighting bulls in areas where no one had ever believed it possible before, controlling the animals to such a degree that he could invade their own terrains.

This diagram illustrates one aspect of the terrain problem, gray indicating the man's terrain and white the bull's. In the case of A the man is exiting from a maneuver into the terrain of the bull. This is known as doing it suerte contraria—contrariwise—going into an area where the bull is naturally inclined to swerve, and hence more dangerous. In B the man is about to kill and go off to the side into his own terrain, since the bull will head away from the fence. This is known as "suerte natural."

(There is no actual demarcation in the arena, of course, and the terrains change with the angle of the bull's body, the position of the man, and their relationship to the circular barrera.)

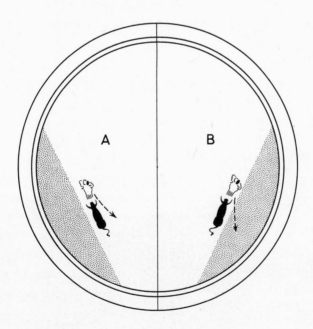

124

There is no set way to commence a faena, since it depends upon the type of bull and the style of the man. However, a very sound way of beginning is with the rough, wrenching passes de castigo—the punishing passes which are designed to gain control over the animal and let him know that this is his sole and final enemy. These trincherazos are functional maneuvers and cannot expect to draw the ecstatic "olés" that the later ornamental passes will merit, but when done with one knee bent gracefully and working close to the bull, it can be a fine sight and the audience will applaud.

Now the matador must unfurl his stylish, statuesque passes. He should plant his feet, lock his knees, straighten his body, and take the bull as close to him as his skill and nerve will permit.

It is hard to see how this pass of Luis Procuna at right could be improved upon for elegance. While very similar to a Pass of Death, it is an invention of the matador himself, known as la procunesa or sanjuanera (after the street

PAGE 98

125

in Mexico City where Procuna used to peddle taco sandwiches before becoming a top "sword"). Wrists crossed, he holds the palillo stick of the muleta in his left hand, the sword in his right, shakes the muleta once or twice to focus the bull's attention on it, and then waits as the animal hurtles toward him. He moves not a muscle, not even turning his head as the horn grazes him, and then he pivots slowly, insolently to the left, barely getting around in time to take the bull's next charge.[1]

If Procuna could do this every day he would be Mexico's top matador. Unfortunately, he is very gypsified. I saw him fight once in Lima in 1946 on the same program with Manolete and Armillita. He had been terrible all season and this day was the last corrida. His first bull was small and charged as though it were on rails, a real "nun," but superstitious Procuna didn't like the way it looked at him with one eye. On the first pass he threw down his cape and dived ignominiously over the fence. Armillita went out with the bull and caped it while not even looking at it, saying, "Look, Luis, there's nothing wrong with this animal—no tiene nada! It charges like silk!"

[1] Sidney Franklin has his own variation of this pass which should be called "la brooklynesa."

PAGE 100

But still Procuna would have nothing to do with it. In the end the animal was led out of the ring alive while the fans screamed their scorn. His next bull was an enormous animal, "a cathedral." Without even waiting to see how it hooked, Procuna ran out in the arena and gave it six kneeling passes. He fought the rest of the fight as though he were trying to commit the most graceful type of suicide ever accomplished, and after dropping the bull with one perfect thrust he was awarded the ears, tail, and one hoof. The delirious crowd swarmed into the ring and carried him on their shoulders through the streets two miles to the stately Bolívar Hotel. When he came downstairs for dinner that evening, everyone in that ultra sophisticated lobby rose as one and applauded, and Luis cried like a baby. Not long ago I saw him do the same thing in Mexico City. After a disastrous season and a disastrous day, during which he was fined 1000 pesos for his disgraceful exhibition, he suddenly decided to buy the substitute bull. After dedicating the bull to the judge who had fined him, he put up what the papers called the next day "possibly the greatest faena ever witnessed in the Plaza Mexico" (below).

But to see Procuna like that once, one has to see him about twenty times

PAGE 101

131

when he does nothing but passes like this one of Villalta's above, left. Compare the yards of safety and this ludicrous stance (a perfectly normal reaction when a bull charges at one, but hardly befitting a star matador with the superb calm and dignity of Manolete above. He is doing a regal pase de la muerte—the pass of death—and as the horn cuts a few inches away from him he manages to look interested but not excited.

The feet do not have to be together for a pass to be elegant and graceful, as this photo at the left of Fuentes Bejarano shows. In fact many bullfighting purists claim that control is sacrificed by keeping the feet together and that the body can not follow through the way it should.

A bullfighter can also start his faena with right-handed passes, like Manolete's on the next page, known as a "derechazo" or "natural with the right hand."

PAGE 103

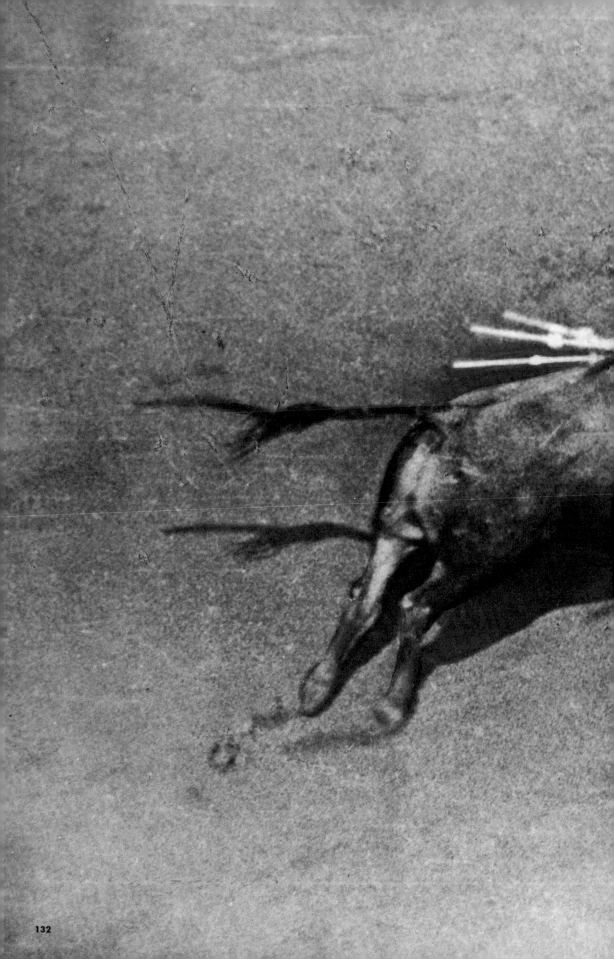

Other opening passes are estatuarios: this languid, statuesque two-handed pass, shown above, and, above right, a sure crowd-pleaser, the dangerous kneeling pase por alto—a one-handed high pass, which can also be done standing up. It is being performed here by Pepín Martín Vásquez when he was only sixteen and the baby-fat still on him. Though from a Sevilla bull-fighting family like Pepe Luis Vásquez, he is no relation.

Another flashy beginning is a pass done while sitting on the estribo—the white stirrup that runs around the bottom of the fence—as Antonio Bien-venida, of the Bienvenida dynasty of toreros, is doing at lower right.

PAGE 106

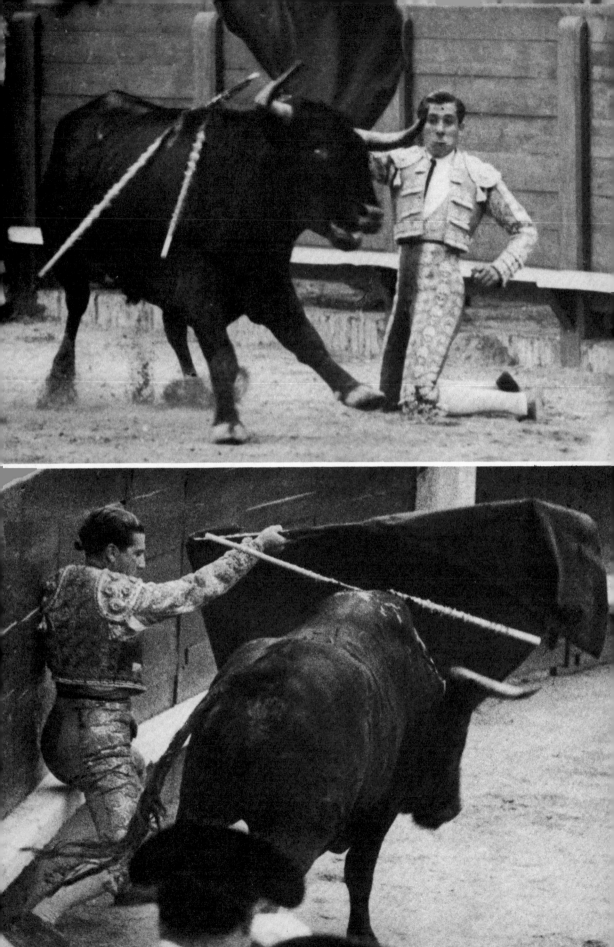

Here the great but erratic Mexican, Silverio Pérez, executes a perfect pase de la firma and when the bull wheels and charges back, he finishes off with a calm pase por alto. This bull was named Tanguito, and because of the magnificent fight he put up that afternoon with Silverio, statues have been erected to him, and he has become one of the most famous bulls in Mexico's history. Sometimes a bull is so tremendously "bravo y noble" that the crowd demands the indulto for him, he is pardoned, and put out to stud. This is a very rare occurrence, however.

PAGE 108

Silverio retired this year after a characteristically disastrous farewell performance in Mexico City. But the public will love him forever for what he did that day with Tanguito. It is incredible that a few brief moments, can be so charged with emotion that they will stay with one, unblurred and exciting, for a lifetime.

PAGE 109

Juan Belmonte is also doing a pase por alto in the top photo, but compare the difference in his and Silverio's style shown on the preceding page; both are superb, and it is merely a question of taste as to which one prefers.

Why the crowd will cheer wildly on one muleta pass and remain silent on another is shown by the two photos below. In the first, the man is yards away from danger, he has no control over the bull, and he is ungraceful. In the second, the man is standing as straight as a ramrod, the bull's head is glued to the muleta, and the bodies are so blended that it looks as though the horn must have gone through the legs.

At the right the bullfighter is demonstrating the cargando la suerte element of a pass—the beautiful following through of the body. Cover the bull with your hand and you still have the record of a highly aesthetic movement. But add the lethal bulk of the bull to the precise delicacy of the man's body and you have a composition of sheer artistry. John Marks writes: ". . . to judge the bullfight otherwise than by an artistic standard is to confuse fundamental issues. . . . Bullfighting is not a cruel sport, but a cruel method of achieving plastic beauty." Belmonte says it is a sexual and spiritual exercise rather than physical.

PAGE 110

142

143

144

Finishing a series of passes, Manolete at the left adjusts the sword in the muleta, his back turned casually to the animal. After a series of pases en redondo—passes in which the bull is lured around the stationary man—he stalks arrogantly away from the animal, as only he could, confident in his judgment that it will not charge at that particular moment.

In the upper photograph at the right, Litri does the pass which Manolete made popular: "mirando al público" (looking at the public while executing a pass).

Since taking one's eye off the bull for even a split second when it is that close is dangerous, this can be classified as a risky maneuver, especially if the matador starts his crowd counting before the horns have passed safely by his legs. This is what happened to a torero who tried this pass without knowing enough about bulls. Look at the photo upside down—the man appears to be holding the bull aloft Atlas-like. This young bullfighter was nicknamed "El Aviador," because he logged so many hours in the air in this manner.

Most horn wounds occur during this last part of the fight. This is because the bull has learned a great deal as the fight has progressed, having charged the cape so many times to no avail, and because the nature of the muleta and the muleta passes

PAGE 113

147

expose the body of the matador more than the large capote does. Often the more spectacular the cogida (the tossing), the less chance there is of its being serious. Sometimes a torero will be tossed twenty feet in the air, alight on the horns, be sent skyward again, and come down only with torn pants, as did the boy above. Another time, below, the bull will barely move its head and drive a horn so deep into a man's leg that he will never walk again. A spectacular and fatal tossing was the death of Granero in 1922 on the horns of the bull Pocapena. The bull gored him through the eye in mid-ring, then carried him in to smash him up against the fence. Lower right, he is taken from the ring already dead, his handsome face destroyed. Granero was Valencia's greatest fighter. He had studied to be a concert violinist, and he was only 20 when the Veragua bull nailed him to the barrera.

PAGE 114

148

149
150

151

1. The torero cites the bull from the right.

Some bullfighters have made great reputations by doing only a few of the classic passes well, such as Mano-lete, who did only the verónica and half-verónica with the cape, and only right- and left-handed naturals, the manoletina, and the Pass of Death with the muleta. But usually the crowds demand variety in the cape-work. The drawings show an exciting variation called the molinete.

Above, Juan Belmonte, the in-ventor of the pass, goes into a moli-nete, the bull putting on the brakes as the cloth lure is snatched from its face. And, below, Belmonte spins out of the molinete.

PAGE 116

2. As the horns pass the legs, the man spins in against the bull's body.

152

3. Revolving as slowly and casu-ally as he dares, he comes around ready to repeat the pass.

The Mexican Armillita saw the old maestro Belmonte do the pass when he first went to Spain and decided to add his own touch—a molinete, but on his knees. Here is a series of molinetes de rodillas done by Arruza. The blood on the costume is not his but the bull's, left there as his body scraped the animal's shoulders.

The danger in any kneeling pass is that if the bullfighter sees the bull is swerving away from the cloth to go at his body, he cannot jump back out of the animal's path as he would if on his feet. Carnicerito demonstrates below what happens when a bull changes his course.

Another spectacular pass is the manoletina, being Manolete's variation of a pass created by La Serna. The muleta and sword are held in the right hand as though for a standard pass, but the left hand goes behind the back and grabs a bit of the cloth. As the bull hits the cloth the man lifts it up over the horns at the same time turning around in the direction the bull has come from. The fighter in the astonishing photo at the left is Miguel del Pino. As he swung the cape up, the bull went up into the air after it. With the camera's stoppage of the action, the bull manages to look like a bovine sleepwalker groping out in front of him with his front legs.

The manoletina is no pass to do with a bull that has a tendency to hook to the right. Joselillo was a brilliant but suicidal twenty-year-old Mexican of a couple of years ago. His tremendous drive to be a great matador led him to take fantastic chances. One day he insisted on doing manoletinas with a bull that hooked radically with its right horn. On the second pass the horn ploughed a deep furrow up the man's leg (top photo) and he died a few days later.

In the lower photo, caught in the same unpleasant manner, Rafael Rodríguez fights the horn with his left hand and gets off with merely a scratch.

PAGE 119

One of the most exciting and dangerous passes is the new "péndulo" pass created by Arruza. The man stands profiled in front of the bull and swings the muleta back and forth behind his legs like a pendulum. With the man's body exposed in the center of the swinging lure, it seems certain that the bull will crash into the man. But Arruza's timing and control over the animal are so perfect that he makes the bull head for the muleta either in front of his body or, what is much more hairraising, *behind* his body.

Automatically the most dangerous pass to attempt in the ring is the arrucina, shown at the foot of the opposite page. The man profiles himself to the bull, holds the muleta and sword behind his leg with his right hand, and offers the bull his choice between the inviting bulk of his shimmering body and the comparatively small area of red rag. It is dangerous for the same reason a kneeling pass is dangerous, i.e., nothing can be done if the bull decides he wants to go at the legs. But in a kneeling pass the man can at least try to distract the bull by holding the muleta away from his body the full length of his arm; with his arm in the arrucina position, the man is helpless until the horn has cut by his body. In the lower left photograph Arruza offers an answer to the question of how-close-can-you-get. In this arrucina below, its inventor has had to go up on his toes and take a deep breath to keep a horn out of him. Passes like this got him called "El Ciclón."

PAGE 121

Now it is time to "go to the left," as Manolo Vásquez is doing above. Although sometimes a matador will begin his faena with left-handed passes, generally he waits until he has done some right-handed work and has the bull well controlled by the muleta. The left-handed pass is basically more dangerous than other passes because the sword does not spread the muleta into a large target. (The left hand never touches the sword during the fight.) Added to the danger of the less alluring size of the muleta, and hence the greater

PAGE 122

likelihood of the bull's going for the man, is the fact that a man's left hand is not usually as adept as his right at the intricacies of manipulation.

The matador begins a natural pass by stalking the bull, chanting to it, and shaking the muleta or hitting it with the sword blade, as you can see Vásquez is doing on the opposite page, to attract the bull's attention away from his completely exposed body.

When the bull charges, the man holds his ground and swings the muleta in front of the animal's snout, as in the lower photo.

That is all there is to "un natural." (Actually it should be called un natural con la izquierda—a natural with the left—so as not to be confused with a natural done with the right hand, but when one refers simply to "un natural," the left-handed pass is meant.)

It is the simplest of passes, like the verónica, but it can be the most beautiful and stylish when done the way Antonio Ordónez is doing at the top of this page.

PAGE 123

Here is perfection, as Manolete executes a natural with a Miura bull in Barcelona in 1944. He was a tall man, yet the huge animal reaches to his chest. The simple, elegant, unfakable natural was Manolete's trademark, and no one could do it better. He did them with his feet together, while the immortal Joselito preferred the stance above, right. Belmonte, below, created a revolutionary style of his own in every pass he did, including the classical natural. Compare the subtle differences of style of the three greats.

Since the bullfighter gets a roar of "olés" and applause for every natural he executes well, he of course tries to do as many as possible. Once in Valencia, Chicuelo gave a bull nineteen historic naturals without a break, a tribute both to the man's skill and the animal's endurance.

PAGE 124

134

When the matador wants to terminate a tanda, or series of naturals, he usually does it with a pase de pecho—a chest pass, which brings the right horn by the man's body instead of the left the way the natural did. At the left, Litri does a superb pase de pecho, the man and bull merging into a monumental composition.

And at the right that same Litri demonstrates the hazards of the pigtailed profession: attempting to do the very same pass in the same fashion, he was slammed to the sand because he forgot it was a different bull—one that had a tendency to hook to the right.

Below, Julio Aparicio shows us what a good pase de pecho looks like from the front while shouting "Olé!" for himself.

ADORNOS

Throughout the faena, the matador will often decorate his work with stunts known as adornos or alardes. These are merely to show his courage and how completely under control he has the bull.

Here Belmonte stands directly in front of the animal and invites it to kill him.

"Mátame, toro," he would shout—Kill me bull, kill me—knowing so much

PAGE 128

about bulls' thinking processes that he was confident it wouldn't charge at that moment.

Above, Joselito gingerly takes hold of a horn with his left hand, but his right has the muleta ready to shove in its face if it should charge. When doing things like this the matador either watches the bull out of the corner of his eye or looks at his banderilleros behind the fence to spot in their faces the warning of any sudden attack. Considered by most experts to be the most technically perfect matador of all time, Joselito once said: "I may be the greatest but Belmonte invented what I do."

PAGE 129

At the top of the opposite page, Arruza does his famous "teléfono" stunt for an adorno, resting his elbow on the bull, with one knee on the ground.

And below he makes it even more dangerous by placing both knees on the ground. Notice his perfect placing of the banderillas.

At the bottom of the opposite page, Litri has cast away his sword and muleta and defies the bull on both knees.

Leaning one's forehead on a bull's horn, above, would seem like the quickest way to commit suicide, but Arruza knows just what he can get away with at this point in the fight.

Showing off like this can be very moving if done with taste and at the right moment, but it also can be overdone. Vulgar stunts like hanging a spectator's hat on a bull's horn can cheapen a matador's entire performance; defying a noble animal is one thing but making it the object of ridicule is quite another.

PAGE 131

ACT VII THE KILL

A faena is made up of a series of passes, it is true, but as Domingo Ortega has said, "dar pases no es lo mismo que torear"—giving passes isn't the same thing as bullfighting. A few isolated passes, no matter how brilliantly executed, do not make up a faena. The passes must have integration, they must be right for that particular bull, the animal must be "brought along" carefully, step by step, the purely ornamental passes must be laid on a firm foundation of functional passes, and the whole performance of this penultimate act should, with increasing excitement and beauty, build and build up to the climax—the kill.

There is no set time for a matador to kill. When he has drawn a very bad bull, he will want to kill as soon as possible after the banderillas, knowing that any fancy capework would be impossible. The fans generally realize that it is a cowardly bull or one with a tendency to go at the man instead of the muleta and excuse the brevity of the faena; the torero usually gives the bull a few "horn-to-horn" punishing passes and then kills.

PAGE 133

When the bull is good, the matador wants to prolong the performance as long as possible, sometimes seven or eight minutes. When he sees that the bull is getting too tired to charge bravely and that it is catching on to the deception of the cloth, he decides to kill.

The first thing the matador must do is cuadrar—to "square" the animal, so that its front feet are together. This opens the shoulder blades and permits the sword to penetrate and cut the aorta artery (the sword rarely hits the heart). If one foot is in front of the other or the feet are too far apart the sword will strike bone and fly out. This is known as a pinchazo.

Here Pepín Martín Vásquez moves around in front of the bull, making it shift its weight and bring its legs together. All in the audience are aware of this feet-together principle. (The other detail which the fans take pride in supervising is when there is a wind blowing the muleta dangerously. "Agua!" they yell, meaning that water should be sprinkled on the cloth to weight it down.)

You will hear the crowd call "No, no!" if the matador starts to "enter" before the bull is right. (It is easier to see that the hoofs are together from the spectator's point of view than from head-on the way the matador looks at the animal.) Once the bull is "squared" the man furls the muleta over the stick, careful to flick the cloth to the right as he does so that the bull will already start thinking ringward and not be given any encouragement to veer fenceward and into the man.

It is ready for the estocada—the sword thrust, and the man is ready for the "moment of truth."

Very rarely one will see a man kill recibiendo, that is, standing still as the bull charges and lets itself be impaled on the sword; but the usual manner of killing is the volapié, literally, "with flying feet."

Sighting down the blade, which is slightly curved so that it will curve down into the vital regions, the bullfighter, leading with the distracting muleta, starts for the animal as it lowers its head to lunge at him.

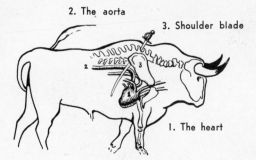

2. The aorta

3. Shoulder blade

1. The heart

How the sword enters the bull's body when correctly placed

"It is the left hand that kills," toreros say, and as the matador throws himself forward, below, he must concentrate not only on hitting the right place with the sword but he must "cross" with his left hand, leading the bull's head under his body as he goes straight over the right horn.

At the right, Manolete's left hand

184

manipulates the muleta so that the bull charges straight and doesn't swerve into the man as the sword arm thrusts the estoque in up to the hilt. If the bull loses interest in the muleta he will lift his head and spike the man in the chest. The estocada is the best chance to get the man that the bull has had all afternoon and hence it is imperative that the man go in to kill straight, passing directly over the right horn. Compare the perfection of Manolete's execution with the shameless assassinations below. It is not much of an accomplishment simply to run off safely to the side of the tired bull and stab it, as the two matadors are doing, and the crowd will let the inept or cowardly matador know what it thinks of him.

PAGE 137

185

186

When the estocada is done well, as above, the man and bull will appear to become one as the sword sinks in. Notice how Arruza's left hand is "crossing" with the muleta—leading the horns under his body. Though the right horn grazed him he was not hurt.

The pictures at left and opposite show what happens if the man fails to cross properly and keep the bull's head down in the muleta.

PAGE 138

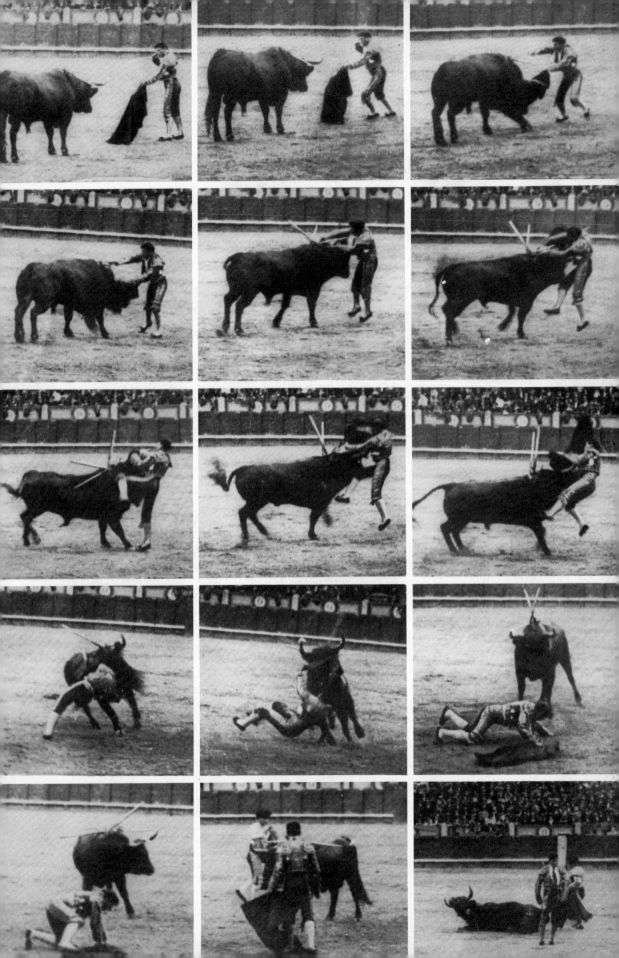

190, 191

In the top photo this novillero has sunk the sword into the withers up to the hilt, but somewhere in the doing he made a mistake and is paying for it. In the lower photo the sword struck shoulder blade, and the power of the bull snaps the man's leg as though it were a breadstick.

PAGE 140

If the man is tossed, the banderilleros rush to his assistance. Below, Manolete lies crumpled, while one peón clings to the bull's tail to distract it and another looks as though he would strangle the animal for having wounded his matador. If not injured, the torero will try to kill again; if he is taken off to the infirmary, the second matador will be obliged to kill the animal. If he is injured, it will go to the third, and in case he too is put out of commission, the animal will be taken out and killed as though it were a beef steer. Corridas are tragedy, for the bull is doomed from the start.

PAGE 141

A sword thrust should not be judged solely by its immediate effect. Sometimes a cowardly thrust will kill the bull immediately. The crowd wants a speedy clean death as much as the matador does, but if he enters to kill honestly each time he will be applauded even if he must try half a dozen times before the animal drops. The regulations state that if the bull is not dead ten minutes after the faena was begun the first warning trumpet is blown. Three minutes later the second aviso is given, and two minutes after that the final one. Then the trained steers—los cabestros—come in to lead the bull out to the slaughterhouse, and the bullfighter is in disgrace.

The most satisfying end to the performance is, of course, for the man to make one perfect sword thrust and have the bull keel over immediately. Here is a study in reactions as three different matadors—Manolete, Belmonte, and Litri—study their fallen adversaries. The crowd cheers when the bull drops, not because "the man has won" or because they like to see an animal die, but simply because to kill correctly the man has risked his life.

Frequently the bull does not go down even after a perfect thrust. The banderilleros will then spin the bull around with their capes so that the sword blade will cut something vital inside; or they will try to drag a cape over the bull's back, catch the pommel with the cloth, and remove the sword so that the rush of air into the wound will kill the animal.

PAGE 142

196, 197

If the bull does not drop and is too beaten to charge for another estocada, the descabello sword is employed (see p. 37). Approaching the sedentary bull, the man keeps the bull's attention focused on the muleta while he jabs the short dagger-like tip of the descabello sword into the nape of the neck. When the spinal cord is severed, the bull crumples, and dies instantly. While anticlimactic, one descabello attempt will not cost the matador an ear if he has put up an otherwise outstanding performance. I have seen Procuna take five sword thrusts and four descabello attempts to kill, all of them clumsy and cowardly, yet the faena that preceded was so incredible, so beautiful, and so moving that he was conceded the ears and tail.

After the *coup de grâce* is administered by the puntillero with a short dagger stroke at the base of the brain, the mules are whipped in fast and chained to the bull's horns. If the animal has put up a fine fight, the crowd will applaud enthusiastically and the vanquished will be given una vuelta— an honorary lap around the ring. If it has put up a cowardly, difficult fight, the crowd will boo lustily, not for the stilled hearing of the bull but for the benefit of the breeder who sent an inferior animal.

In any case, the bull is dragged out of the ring to be butchered, the dragging-out process being known as el arrastre.[1] (In Mexico the meat is usually given to the poor, while in most Spanish rings the surprisingly tender steaks are sold right at the arena.)

[1] The finest arrastre I ever witnessed was when an amateur torero friend of mine fought in a festival fight near Barcelona when very drunk. After performing numerous unintentional novelties, such as placing a pair of banderillas in a fellow performer's shoulders instead of in the bull's, he climaxed the debacle by tripping over the dead bull during the arrastre and was dragged out *hors de combat* on top of his victim. The sad part of it all was that he had arranged the fight to impress his fiancée and her family, who never spoke to him again.

So now the bull is dead, and if he had the power to choose, which death would he have chosen: the abattoir where the smell of unresisted slaughter seeps in to all the pathetic herded creatures before the clumsy, meaningless slugging? Or this fiery, hot-blooded contest where he is sure he is winning right up to the last moment?

PAGE 145

200

Now it is the man's turn to be applauded or booed. In this case, a young novillero who expected to win fame and glory by his first fight in Sevilla's big ring received boos for his failure to kill; he sobs against the barrera while his banderillero glares at the insults his matador is taking.

In Mexico the spectators are more violent. It is not unusual for irate fans to express their disapproval by piling cushions together and burning them. Sometimes there is a division of opinions, part of the audience applauding and the others booing, thinking the torero could have done more. Once Rafael el Gallo, after a terrible fight of his, was asked how it went. "División de opiniones," mumbled the gypsy. "Yes," his manager explained, "there was a division of opinions—half the people called you a dirty coward and the other half a clumsy bum."

If the bullfighter has put up a good fight but has had to take two or three sword thrusts to kill, the crowd will still applaud, and if the applause is prolonged enough he will take a lap around the ring (clockwise in Spain, counterclockwise in Mexico). The enthusiastic crowd will throw cigars, hats, and wineskins down to the matador. His men, trailing behind him, keep the cigars, help skim the hats back, and toss back the wineskins after the matador has either taken or pantomimed a squirt of manzanilla. I have seen a wooden leg, a pair of women's panties, and a baby tossed into the ring by delirious crowds. (In the case of the baby, the torero put it on his shoulders and gave it a lap around, the wooden leg went back to its owner, and the panties were tucked into the man's shirt next to his heart.)

If the bullfighter has put up a very good performance with the cape and muleta and killed well, the crowd indicates by waving handkerchiefs and shouting "Oreja" that they want the presidente to concede an ear before the bull is dragged out. If there are enough handkerchiefs, the presidente will indicate by producing his handkerchief that he awards an ear. (This custom started back in the days when bullfighters weren't so rich and the ear entitled them to the meat of the animal.) If the clamor keeps up he will award both ears, and if it still persists, the tail, and very very rarely, a hoof. A banderillero cuts the appendages from the dead animal and hands them to his matador, who runs around the ring holding them aloft and finally tosses them to the

crowd, like Arruza, below. Sometimes energetic admirers carry the
matador around on their shoulders,
like Domínguín, right, but usually
this is reserved until after the last
bull.

Here a wounded matador, El Estudiante, has been brought the ears and tail of his dead adversary, but he has keeled over into the arms of his banderilleros and is carried to the infirmary instead of taking a triumphal lap. A Spaniard likened this dramatic photo to the Descent from the Cross.

A matador sometimes will have to make two or three laps around the ring and then walk to los medios—as the great Juan Belmonte is doing at the right. Standing there in the center of the ring, he takes the thunderous ovation which the audience accords to a brave, artistic, performer.

But he does not stay there long, for soon a trumpet blows. It reminds him and the crowd that there are more bulls still to be fought this afternoon. In a moment one of them will burst into the sun of the arena looking for something to kill, and another brave man will accept the challenge.

PAGE 148

203

GREAT
MATADORS
OF THIS
CENTURY

THE FIRST MAN of importance to take the alternative and become a full matador in the twentieth century was Rafael el Gallo—the Rooster. He was a prematurely bald, colorful, unpredictable gypsy from Sevilla who was as famous for his "espantás" (his sudden frightened fleeings) as he was for his great faenas. In thirty years as a matador he was never gored seriously. Once when he came home with a slight leg wound his mother is supposed to have asked: "But how did it happen, Rafaé'—did the bull jump over the fence after you?"

There are hundreds of anecdotes about El Divino Calvo—The Divine Bald One—and so many of them are about his superstitions, irregularities, and periodic cowardice that the fact that he was a great torero is sometimes dimmed. Nowadays, aged 71 he holds court in the Gallango or Los Corales cafés in Sevilla, as in the photo at left. With his sombrero cordobés and smoking his ever present "puro" like the true flamenco he is, he reminisces about his ring rivals like Bombita and Machaquito—and his brother, Joselito.

From the time he was a young boy, it was clear that Joselito, "Little José," was a genius. Starting at thirteen to fight professionally as a becerrista—a calf fighter—he amazed everyone who saw him perform. It was as though he had nothing to learn—that he instinctively knew everything that went on in a bull ring. An athlete, he placed his own banderillas, killed perfectly, and swung a cape with more grace and surety than had yet been seen.

In 1912, before his seventeenth birthday, Joselito received the alternative from his brother, at right, and became a full matador de toros, the youngest ever to wear that title.

PAGE 153

207

All Spain was excited about the handsome prodigy, above, who could dominate any bull that came into the ring. Only the Mexican master, Gaona (below), could be mentioned in the same breath with Joselito. (Named José Gómez, he was called Joselito el Gallo or Gallito.)

And then along came another genius from Sevilla, Juan Belmonte. Instead of being tall and good-looking, he was little and bandy-legged and ugly, and he stammered. Unlike Joselito, whose cousins, brother, and father were all established matadors (one day there were thirteen members of the family fighting in different rings), no one in Juan Belmonte's family had ever been connected with bullfighting. One of eleven children and wretchedly poor, Belmonte didn't get a real chance at bullfighting until he was 18. Then he was a complete failure, virtually laughed out of the ring, and he had to go to work as a day laborer. But there was something in this sickly youth that made him try again and again; like Manolete, he had a yearning to be great, a *having* to be somebody. He wangled a few minor fights. And soon people were talking about him, telling their friends to go see this

208

PAGE 154

little mushroom of a man with the strange suicidal style. "If you haven't seen this Belmonte, you'd better hurry!" the experts said significantly.

His style was completely unorthodox, but very moving. The accepted rule for el torero had always been: "You place yourself there, and when the bull charges you either move yourself in a hurry or it'll do the moving for you." Belmonte thought it made better sense to stay right where he was and, with his skillful wrists controlling the cape, make the bull get out of his way. They say it was his physical handicaps which forced him to create this new style, that he was unable to dance out of the way of the bulls and had to make them go around him. "My legs were in such a state," he once said, "that if one desired to move it had to request permission from the other."

Joselito quickly adapted himself to this revolutionary style, and together they formed the greatest pair the bull ring has ever seen: Joselito the Invincible (above), who was never tossed, who would kill six bulls by himself in an afternoon and ask for the substitute bull to make it seven; Joselito the Perfect, about whom they said there was no heifer who could drop the bull that could hurt him, who never made a mistake in the ring, who

PAGE 155

made every maneuver look easy. And Belmonte, the creator (above), the big-jawed little revolutionist who had changed a centuries-old spectacle over night, hobbling out against bulls that came to his shoulder, fighting on guts alone, taking them in impossible terrains, getting tossed nearly every afternoon but doing the most incredible things that a man had ever done with bulls.

Belmonte and Joselito fought side by side for eight years, a period that is known as The Golden Age of Bullfighting. Inside the arena they were the greatest rivals, but outside they were best friends. Every season Joselito grew more perfect and secure in the ring, and every year, the experts said, would be Belmonte's last.

"To die, Juanito," a writer friend once remarked, "all you have left to do is to die gloriously in the arena."

"I'll do my best," Belmonte countered.

And that's what it looked like, for instead of his ardor cooling with his wealth and fame it seemed he had never fought so suicidally.

But it wasn't Belmonte who was killed.

On May 16, 1920, in the little town of Talavera de la Reina, a scrawny, substitute bull named Bailaor (Dancer) ripped open Joselito's stomach as he was changing his grip on the muleta. He died almost immediately, gasping, "Mother, I'm smothering, I'm smothering!" He was 24 years old.

Belmonte was home resting after an injury when they telephoned to tell him that his best friend had been killed. He laughed and said "Impossible!"

and hung up. Then he learned the truth. "I was held speechless . . . and wept as I had never wept before," he says in *Juan Belmonte, Killer of Bulls,* his autobiography as told to Manuel Chaves Nogales, translated into English by Leslie Charteris. "I think I felt a little of my own death that day; and this egotistical reflection was what gave me strength to pull myself together."

Two days later in the Madrid ring he put up the greatest show of daring of his entire career.

But after Joselito was buried under a huge bronze and marble tomb depicting nineteen life-size figures bearing the torero's coffin, Belmonte announced his retirement. He could stay away from the rings only two years, however, before making a triumphal comeback. He retired again and came back again, greater than ever.

Now 62, he lives on his large estate near Sevilla, where he raises fighting bulls for younger men to fight. He has everything—wealth, the adulation of the nation, grandchildren, everything that Manolete sacrificed to the horns of Islero. But Don Juan cannot stay away from the bulls. The living room opens on to his small bull ring and he cannot resist getting down in the arena to once more hypnotize the horny tribe with his magic cape. And when he does, even at his age, I swear there is no one in the world who can compete with him. He fights a few big charity fights a year also,

PAGE 157

starting out Portuguese style (preceding page). This is an attractive ramification of bullfighting occasionally seen. The opposite of the picador's job, it consists of a skilled horseman maneuvering his highly trained horse to avoid the bull's charges while placing banderillas and ultimately killing.

When I appeared on the same program with Belmonte in 1945, the bull he fought in this way was immense. Instead of killing it from horseback, however, he dismounted, and with the sword and muleta he put up the most exciting performance I have ever seen. The next day the headlines of the taurine section shouted: WE HAVE SEEN WHAT IT IS TO FIGHT A BULL! and then went on to say, "Incredible as it seems, Juan Belmonte is fighting better than anyone in the ring today."

He is undoubtedly the most revered Spaniard. He explains it in his autobiography. "To every Spaniard I was part of himself. Those who hoped to make a success of life looked at me as a mirror of their own future success. Those waging a losing struggle for existence remembered that I had been even more handicapped and had overcome my handicaps. Those aware of being ugly and misshapen consoled themselves with my ugliness and misshapenness. They looked at me and saw me so feeble, so insignificant, so opposite from what one would expect a conquering hero to be, that their own weaknesses seemed much less of an obstacle to overcome."

After Joselito's death and Belmonte's first retirement, Manuel Jiménez, "Chicuelo," below, was the king pin. An inventive stylist with the cape and muleta, he was a poor killer and an uneven performer.

PAGE 158

A very sure if uninspired rival was the highly competent Marcial Lalanda, above, who for twenty years was a top figure in Spain.

The erratic young gypsy, Cagancho, below, took the alternative from the erratic old gypsy, El Gallo, in 1927 and became known as a bullfighter's bullfighter. Sunday after Sunday he would drive the crowds to fury with his cowardice, but then when he conquered his superstitions and fear he would put up a performance of such unbelievable gypsy grace that he would have the other matadors green with envy.

PAGE 159

Mexico's first great contribution to the ring since Gaona was Fermín Espinosa, "Armillita," shown above. Cold, scientific, versatile, he went to the top rung when he was 16 and stayed there for 25 years, a modern record. Because of his versatility, he was what is known as a torero largo like Joselito, as opposed to a torero corto, or limited fighter. He was gored only once in his career and that was the year before his retirement.

Domingo Ortega, below, who took his alternative in 1931, dominated the Spanish bull world for almost ten years with his artistry. He had a tremendous ability to control any bull that came out of the toril and gear down their charges with his superb *temple*. A waiter from Borox, Spain, Ortega took up bullfighting at a comparatively advanced age, becoming a matador at 25. He has managed to make a lot of money, marry two marquesas, and is now a successful breeder of bulls. Except for Manolo Bienvenida and the Mexicans Balderas and Garza, his competition was slight until the advent of Manolete, shown resting between bulls here, in 1939.

PAGE 160

Then he had to take a back seat, for bullfighting, which had been in the doldrums for the previous decade, saw a new renaissance because of the genius of Manolete's style and the honesty he brought with him to every arena. Known as El Monstruo, he was called, along with Belmonte and Joselito, one of the three greatest bullfighters of all time.

He was immediately paired off with Pepe Luis Vásquez, left, whose exciting, florid, varied Sevillan style ("alegría" they call it—"gaiety") contrasted perfectly with Manolete's cold Cordovan austerity. Unfortunately, early in their rivalry, Pepe Luis received a bad goring in which he almost lost an eye, and he never regained the confidence he had. "If it were my leg, it wouldn't be so bad," he says, "but every time I look in the mirror I see my destroyed face and I am afraid." However, when he feels like it he is still capable of putting up as elegant, moving, and technically perfect a performance with cape and muleta as can be seen.

Carlos Arruza, lower left, took Spain by storm in 1944 and *the* program for the next three years was Manolete vs. Arruza. Like Joselito and Belmonte, Arruza and Manolete were friends out of the arena, and after Islero spiked the Cordovan and put him in his marble sarcophagus,
PAGE 162

Arruza "cut the pigtail." (Cutting the pigtail used to be the last ceremonial act of a torero's professional career. They say that the Chinese matador, Vicente Hong, was the only bullfighter to *begin* his career by cutting the pigtail.)

He married and intended to stay retired forever on his ranch in Sevilla, but he only lasted three years without the roar of "olé" in his ears. When he came back he was greater than he had ever been, and now at 33 he is considered by most bullfighters and experts to be the greatest living bullfighter.

There is no argument that he is the greatest banderillero. Although his verónicas are undistinguished, he has a great repertoire in the *quites* and with the muleta he is able to work his extraordinary, hypnotic domination on almost every bull he encounters.

The greatest performance I've ever seen was Arruza's in Málaga in 1945. Incredible with the cape and the sticks, he was even better with the muleta. Once he was tossed, and to save himself he wrapped his arms around the bull's neck and clung to it. Seconds later he casually rested his forehead on the bull's horn. After a perfect kill, the crowd set up a clamor until he had been awarded ears, tail, hooves—and finally, the whole bull!

PAGE 163

Arruza's greatest rival for the title of Number One is Luis Miguel Domin-guín, shown at left and below. A prodigy of the arena, Dominguín has been fighting professionally since he was 12 years old and at 27 he was at the top. The son and brother of bullfighters, Dominguín owns many of Spain's bull rings. He is un torero largo, since he is equally good with cape, bande-rillas, muleta, and sword. Coldly perfect in the ring, confident and cocky, Dominguín's prowess is recognized by the crowds, but he is considered "antipático" compared to the simpático Arruza.

While millionaires Dominguín and Arruza are the "colósos" of the arenas today, both have announced their retirements. Recently I saw Arruza put up a truly superb fight in Mexico City, and then, as the crowd chanted their highest tribute, "Tor-er-o!" he reached up and pulled off his pigtail to sym-bolize that they had watched him cut ears and tail for the last time. Whether or not Arruza can stay away and Dominguín makes good his boast to quit there are many fine young toreros around eager to try to take their places. This year's most promising stars seem to be Ordóñez, Jumillano, Pedrés, and Juan Belmonte III (a nephew), already being hailed as "fenómenos," although they are all under twenty. Probably one of them, if he does not have the bad fortune to encounter his own Islero, or lose his nerve through a bad goring, will some day be "El Número Uno" of all Spain.

PAGE 165

THE DISTAFF SIDE

Surprising as it seems, I receive hundreds of letters a year from Americans wanting to become bullfighters and seeking information as to how to achieve this goal. I would guess that half of the letters come from young women.

With the males I am most discouraging, pointing out that it is extremely difficult for a Spaniard to make his way in the bull world even if he comes from a bullfighting family and has great connections. For a female of any nationality, it is virtually impossible. Conchita Cintrón is a phenomenon.

Now retired at 31, she is the only woman bullfighter who has ever been worthy of the name "torera," and even she was not allowed to compete on foot with men in Spain, mainly because she was so very good. As one matador said: "After the crowd sees a girl put up such a good show, you have to go out there and eat the bull alive to get any applause."

Like the great rejoneador Cañero, Conchita would start out "Portuguese style" on horseback. After a superb display of horsemanship, during which she would place banderillas and rejones, she would dismount and take the animal on with muleta and sword. (She was allowed to dismount only in Latin America.) A
PAGE 166

224, 225
226

slim, good-looking young woman, Conchita was born of a Puerto Rican father and an Irish-American mother in Chile. Brought up in Peru, where her father was an employee of the American embassy, she left the fashionable school she attended to study horsemanship and the art of rejoneo under the Portuguese riding master, Ruy da Camara. Fighting on foot followed after she made several successful appearances as a rejoneadora before regular fights in Mexico, and she immediately became a star.

One of the greatest exponents of the art of "Portuguese fighting" (not to be confused with the emasculated, non-killing type of corrida found in Portugal), Conchita was also a highly competent fighter on foot. She is the only woman, including all Texas and Mexican candidates, to be regarded seriously in the annals of tauromachy.

WHERE AND WHEN TO SEE THEM

Mexico's season of corridas formales, the big fights, is from November to March. During the summer the novilladas, featuring the apprentice fighters, take place. Peru's temporada begins the end of October. Bullfights in Latin America observe the same basic pattern and traditions as in Spain.

Spain's season starts the end of March with the Falleras fights in Valencia's fair, continuing until the end of October. Unlike Mexico, the novilladas and the big corridas take place during the same season.

The most important dates on the taurine calendar in Spain are: the fair at Sevilla (below), which starts April 18 and runs for seven days, the fair of San Isidro in Madrid in May, the Pamplona fair, July 7, and the fair of Bilbao the middle of August. In Madrid you will see the biggest bulls.

The Pamplona fair is famous and justly so, for nowhere else is there a town whose entire male population is made up of maniacs. Every year they barricade the side streets and turn loose the bulls which are to be fought that afternoon by professionals. The young men of the city then run in front of the animals in an attempt to reach the ring a mile away. Usually there are fatalities and dozens of injured, but the encierro ritual goes on happily for five days. Once the mayor

PAGE 167

of the town declared the pastime barbarous and outlawed it, whereupon the outraged citizenry, defending their inalienable right to self-maim, clapped the mayor in jail and left him there until the fiesta was over.

Above, a bull has caught up with one Pamplonica and is trying to gore him while a friend bravely tries to make the *quite* by swerving in and distracting the animal. Notice the wonderful impersonation of a gutter the man in the background is giving. Next a finely composed picture is made as a bull knocks one runner flat and swerves off after several others.

Below, a bull has burst through the barrier and seems certain to gore the little girl who is running to her mother (on her knees at the left). The bull missed the girl but gored her mother, who lies in the street while the bull holds the crowd at bay and decides whom to charge next. The Guardia Civil arrived a few seconds after this picture was taken and shot the animal.

Coming into the bull ring (opposite page) is the most dangerous part of the run, for when the dozens of frantic runners try to get through the narrow passageway at once there is bound to be a jam-up. In the amorphous mass on pages 170 and 171 there can be found eight animals, the black and white ones being the trained steers. Once in the ring, the runners jump over the fence and climb up into the stands to safety.

While highly exciting, the much publicized encierros of Pamplona should not be classified as bullfighting; they are a ridiculous aberration of la fiesta

PAGE 168

brava, with no aesthetic end achieved by the participants to atone for the brutality and danger involved.

Pamplona has a mad fascination. It is probably the best evidence of the tremendous basic appeal of man's quixotic desire to pit himself against an overwhelming living force. As such it is perhaps the ultimate expression of the brutal core of all fights between man and bull.

But the real corrida—la corrida formal—transcends the simple struggle of bull and man. It is in fact a religious ceremony, a reverent blood sacrifice from which still curls the smoke of ancient altars. If one wanted to get gaudy, one could say that standing beside the Manoletes who deliberately expose themselves to their murderous Isleros is a shadowy figure old as the human race: the priestly slayer of Attis the Bull God, who is the incarnation of the Life Force and who must be killed in order that his strength may be preserved. In a time when the common sense of deductive science makes even the churches materialistic, the splendid, unreasonable, anacronistic man-testing ritual of a bullfight springs directly from the deepest mysteries of the human soul.

John Steinbeck summed it up succinctly when he wrote in a recent letter: "I like bullfights, because to me it is a lonely, formal, anguished microcosm of what happens to every man, sometimes even in an office, strangled by the glue on envelopes. In the bull ring he survives for a while sometimes. There's a fierce, unbeaten acceptance of final defeat in the bull ring and I love gallantry above all virtues. It is the prime virtue of the individual and the only occidental invention, and being lost, the individual gets lost."

GLOSSARY

An attempt is made to indicate the phonetic pronunciation after each word. The Andaluz accent is used rather than Castilian, hence the *c*'s and *z*'s are not lisped. Actually, the Andaluz, with characteristic perversity, chooses to lisp his *s*'s as well as to swallow the endings of words, and so "sí señor" comes out "thee then·yoh." However, a high order of Andaluz is approximated here which is like well-spoken Mexican Spanish. Some contend that good Mexican is the purest Spanish spoken. In both Spain and Latin America *r*'s beginning a word, as well as double *r*'s, are trilled, the *d*'s in most words ending in *do* or *da* are softened to the point of sounding closer to "tho" and "tha" than to a hard *d;* and *v*'s are softened to be indistinguishable from *b*'s. The italicized syllable is the one to be stressed.

COMMON TERMS FOR THE DIFFERENT COLORINGS
OF FIGHTING BULLS

While aficionados traditionally prefer their bulls black, bulls of variations and mixtures of red, white, and black are fought in every plaza in every country. The color of a bull tells one nothing about what kind of a performance it will put up, but every true aficionado is vitally interested in the bull's "estampa"— his coat, markings, and general physical appearance. I don't believe there is anything comparable in American livestock breeding to the complexity of the variations indicated by these terms that are everyday words to the aficionado.

albahio (ahl·*bah*·yoh) yellowish white

aldinegro (ahl·dee·*nay*·groh) a chestnut or red bull with black underbody, including head and feet

anteado (ahn·tay·*ah*·thoh) light red with dark spots

aparejado (ah·pahr·ray·*hah*·thoh) a pinto whose spots run more or less symmetrically on both sides of its backbone

asarajado (ah·sah·rah·*hah*·thoh) tawny, like a lion

azabache (ah·sah·*bah*·chay) shiny, velvety black

barroso (bah·*roh*·soh) dirty white

berrendo (bayr·*rayn*·thoh) white with spots of another color—either chestnut, red, or black

bociblanco (boh·see·*blahng*·coh) bull with white muzzle

bocinegro or bocinero (boh·see·*nay*·groh) bull with black muzzle

botinero (boh·tee·*nay*·roh) light-colored, with dark-colored legs

bragado (brah·*gah*·thoh) bull of any color but with white stomach

calcetero (cahl·say·*tay*·roh) dark-colored bull with white feet

capirote (cah·pee·*roh*·tay) when head is a different color from body

capuchino (cah·poo·*chee*·noh) like capirote marking except that the different coloring comes to a point on neck; rare

castaño (cahs·*tahn*·yoh) chestnut

cárdeno (*cahr*·then·oh) gray

careto (cah·*ray*·toh) bull of any coloring but with face or forehead of a different coloring

caribello (cahr·ree·*bayl*·yoh) bull whose face or forehead has white hairs but not solid enough to form a spot

carifosco (cahr·ree·*fohs*·coh) bull with curly hair on crown of head

carinegro (cahr·ree·*nay*·groh) any chestnut, red, or gray bull with black face

carinevado (cahr·ree·nay·*bah*·thoh) like caribello

caripintado (cahr·ree·peen·*tah*·thoh) bull with spots on face of different color from rest of body

carivacado (cahr·ree·bah·*cah*·thoh) bull with an elongated snout

coliblanco (coh·lee·*blahng*·coh) bull of any color with white tail

colorado (coh·lor·*rah*·thoh) deep red

chorreado (chore·ray·*ah*·thoh) bull with vertical stripes of a darker hue than its basic color

ensabonado (en·sah·bohn·*ah*·thoh) dirty white

entrepelado (en·tray·pay·*lah*·thoh) black with some white hairs but not quite gray

estornino (ace·tohr·*nee*·noh) black with little spots of another color, but very few

estrellado (ace·trayl·*yah*·thoh) bull with spot on forehead darker than rest of body

gijón or jijón (hee·*hone*) bull of flaming red

jabonero (hah·boh·*nay*·roh) soapy white, *café au lait*

jirón or girón (hee·*rone*) bull of solid color with one single white patch on any part of body except head or stomach

lomipardo, also written lombardo or lompardo (loh·mee·*pahr*·thoh) black with brown loins

lucero (loo·*say*·roh) literally, the morning star; bull of any color with white spot on forehead

meleno (may·*lay*·noh) bull with a lock of hair hanging down over forehead melocotón (may·loh·coh·*tone*) peach-colored bull

mohino or mojino (moh·*ee*·noh) bull with black muzzle

mulato (moo·*lah*·toh) bull of dull-black and gray

nevado (nay·*bah*·thoh) "snowed upon"; bull of any color with small white spots all over

ojalao (oh·hah·*lah*·oh) bull with light circle around eyes

ojinegro (oh·hee·*nay*·groh) bull with a dark circle around eyes

ojo de perdiz (*oh*·hoh day pare·*dees*) "partridge-eyed"; a red circle around eyes

pardo (*pahr*·thoh) dark grayish brown

pajizo (pah·*hee*·soh) yellow, straw-colored bull

perlino (pare·*lee*·noh) light pearly gray

rabicano (rah·bee·*cah*·noh) tail with some white bristles in it

rabicorto (rah·bee·*cohr*·toh) short-tailed

rabilargo (rah·bee·*lahr*·goh) long-tailed

rabón (rah·*bone*) tailless bull, like Tom Lea's Brujo in *The Brave Bulls*

rebarbo (ray·*bahr*·boh) dark head and light muzzle

retinto (ray·*teen*·toh) red bull of varying degrees of redness, as though dyed twice in different shades

salinero (sah·lee·*nay*·roh) chestnut with white hairs throughout

salpicado (sahl·pee·*cah*·thoh) like nevado but with fewer and larger white spots

sardo (*sahr*·thoh) a mixture of black, red, and white hairs

zaino (sah·*ee*·noh) jet black, but not shiny like azabache

THE HORNS

The most important thing about a bull's make-up, to the matador, is its armament. Small two-year-old calves have almost killed such ring greats as Belmonte and Ortega with their needlelike little horns. Bailaor, the bull that killed Joselito, was little more than a calf, but its horns were perfect for killing.

What the matador wants is a "comfortable head," i.e., the horns neither spread too far out nor curved too far in. Of the two, he will prefer the latter, for although once the very curved horn is in the man's flesh it is harder to get out, there is also less chance of his getting hooked in the first place. The modern breeder tries to breed for small horns and comfortable ones.

When the banderillero comes back to his matador from the drawing of the animals, the first thing he is asked is to describe the horns of the two "bichos," their size, sharpness, and shape. There is an extensive vocabulary for this part of tauromachy alone, of which a partial list follows:

abierto de cuerno (ah·bee·*yer*·toh day coo·*air*·noh) wide-horned

astiagudo (ah·stee·ah·*goo*·thoh) sharp-pointed horns

astiblanco (ahs·tee·*blahng*·coh) horns that are nearly all-white

astifino (ah·stee·*fee*·noh) thin, polished horns

astigordo, also cornigordo (ahs·tee·*gohr*·thoh) thick-horned

astillado (ahs·teel·*yah*·thoh) horns splintered at end

astillano (ahs·teel·*yah*·noh) horns with practically no curve

astinegro (ahs·tee·*nay*·groh) completely black horns

astisucio (ahs·tee·*soo*·see·yoh) horns of dirty-white coloring

astiverde (ahs·tee·*bare*·they) greenish horns

bizco (*bees*·coh) literally, cross-eyed; but used to designate a bull with one horn higher than the other, the lower horn being referred to as the bizco one in specific use, i.e., "bizco of the left"

brocho (*broh*·choh) horns curved very close together

capacho (cah·*pah*·choh) wide and drooping horns

cornalón (cohr·nah·*lone*) bull with tremendous horns

cornialto (cohr·nee·*ahl*·toh) long- and high-horned

corniancho (cohr·nee·*ahn*·choh) same as abierto de cuerno

corniapretado (cohr·nee·ah·pray·*tah*·thoh) horns close together like the brocho

cornigacho (cohr·nee·*gah*·choh) horns that start from head lower than usual and curve downward

cornipaso (cohr·nee·*pah*·soh) horns whose points curve out to side

cornitrasero (cohr·nee·trah·*say*·roh) horns starting farther back than usual

cornivacado (cohr·nee·bah·*cah*·thoh) cowlike horns that jut out almost perpendicularly from head

cornivicioso (cohr·nee·bee·see·*oh*·soh) any defective horns

cornivuelto (cohr·nee·boo·*el*·toh) horns whose tips curve backward

cubeto (coo·*bay*·toh) drooping horns whose points almost touch

mocho (*moh*·choh) bull so blunt and short of horn to be virtually hornless

mogón (moh·*gohn*) bull with one or both horns blunted or crumpled

ELEMENTARY GLOSSARY OF BULLFIGHTING TERMS

achuchón (ah·choo·*chone*) a bumping by the bull suffered by the man

acoso (ah·*coh*·soh) pursuing young animals with blunted lance (p. 18)

adorno (ah·*thor*·noh) any embellishing maneuver (p. 128)

afeitar (ah·fay·*tahr*) to shave, dock bull's horns (p. 50)

afición (ah·fee·see·*own*) love for "los toros"—bullfighting; also refers to discriminating aficionados as a group, viz., "The novillero was hailed by la afición as a veritable phenomenon"

aficionado (ah·fee·see·own·*ah*·thoh) rabid fan; also amateur torero

agotado (ah·go·*tah*·thoh) refers to a bull exhausted by combat

aguantar (ah·wan·*tahr*) means to withstand or stick it out, as when a bull dangerously stops halfway through a charge and the man refuses to give ground, waiting out rest of charge

aire (ah·*ee*·ray) means the wind, dreaded by toreros because the capes become unmanageable; many bullfighters have been gored when the wind blew the cape or muleta across their legs

al alimón (ahl ah·lee·*mone*) very safe pass where two people hold opposite ends of the capote and let the bull charge between; only seen now at tientas, where it is generally done by a bullfighter and a squealing girl friend

alarde (ah·*lahr*·they) see *adorno*

alegría (ah·lay·*gree*·ah) gaiety and variety of style in the ring (p. 162)

alguacil (ahl·wah·*ceel*) mounted constable who rides at head of bullfighters as they parade into ring; he transmits any orders of the presidente to the bullfighters during fight (p. 36)

alino (ah·*lee*·noh) a faena de alino is one where the bullfighter limits himself to a few functional passes, letting any fancy stuff go by, and lines up bull to kill as soon as possible

alternativa (ahl·ter·nah·*tee*·vah) ceremony where a matador de novillos graduates to a matador de toros (p. 36)

alto (*ahl*·toh) when a sword thrust is "en todo lo alto," it has been placed right in the "cross" (see *cruz*)

alto, pase por (*ahl*·toh, *pah*·say pohr) muleta pass (p. 106)

aplomado (ah·plom·*ah*·thoh) leaden: the bull's state toward end of fight

apoderado (ah·poh·they·*rah*·thoh) matador's manager; generally receives 5 per cent of his sword's fee

apodo (ah·*poh*·thoh) nickname, such as "Niño de Triana"—"Kid from Triana"

aprovechando del viaje (ah·pro·bay·*chahn*·doh del bee·*ah*·hay) taking advantage of the trip (p. 97)

arajai (ah·rah·*hi*) gypsy term for "priest." Many toreros have died in the ring before "un arajai" could be fetched. There are always gitanos in bullfighting, and many "caló" expressions are affected by non-gypsies in the profession

arrancada (ah·rahn·*cah*·thah) the bull's charge

arrastre (ah·*rahs*·tray) removal of bull from arena (p. 144)

arrimarse (ahr·ree·*mahr*·say) to work close to bull

arroba (ah·*roh*·bah) about 25 pounds; bull-folk usually estimate weight of bulls in arrobas

arrucina (ah·roo·*see*·nah) muleta pass of Carlos Arruza's invention (p. 121)

asta (*ahs*·tah) another word for horn

astado (ahs·*tah*·thoh) another word for bull

aviso (ah·*bee*·soh) warning trumpet (p. 142)

ayudado (ah·yoo·*dah*·thoh) un pase ayudado is any pass where the muleta is "helped" with the sword

bajonazo (bah·hoh·*nah*·soh) a safe unfair sword thrust low on neck

banderillas (bahn·day·*reel*·yahs) barbed sticks (pp. 37, 85)

banderillas de fuego (bahn·day·*reel*·yahs day foo·*ay*·goh) banderillas with firecrackers attached, used to enliven a bull reluctant to charge picadors; outlawed since 1950; now supplanted by the "black banderillas," ones with larger points than usual

barrera (bah·*ray*·rah) red wooden fence around arena; also, first rows in stands are known as "barreras"

basto (*bah*·stoh) clumsy

becerro (bay·*sayr*·roh) calf, up to three years. Within that classification: añojo (yearling), eral (two-year-old), and utrero (between two and three)

bicho (*bee*·choh) bug, beast; slang for bull

boleto (boh·*lay*·toh) ticket for bull ring in Mexico; billete (beel·*yay*·tay) is the word in Spain

bramar (brah·*mahr*) to bellow; the bull that bellows excessively is usually cowardly

bravo (*brah*·boh) wild; "un toro bravo" means a wild, fighting bull in generic sense rather than simply "a brave bull" as opposed to a cowardly one (p. 14)

bravucón (brah·voo·*cohn*) bull that makes a show of bravery but turns out cowardly

brindis (*breen*·dees) dedication (p. 95)

bruto (*broo*·toh) "en bruto" is weighing of bull before it is dressed (see *canal*)

buey (boo·*way*) ox; opprobrious term for the bull

burel (boo·*rayl*) gypsy term for bull

burladero (boor·lah·*they*·roh) shield in front of fence openings (p. 32)

cabestros (cah·*bays*·trohs) the trained steers leading bulls from arena if matador fails to kill (p. 142)

cajón (cah·*hone*) reinforced crate in which bull is shipped, two meters high, two and a half long, and too narrow for bull to turn around in (p. 22)

calé (cah·*lay*) gypsy word for anything gypsy

callejón (cahl·yay·*hone*) passageway between fence and the stand (p. 32)

caló (cah·*loh*) the gypsy language, many terms of which are used in la fiesta brava

cambio (*cahm*·bee·oh) change; to change bull's direction of charge after it has once attacked is always dangerous. Among the maneuvers based on the cambio are banderillas al quiebro and the larga cambiada pass (pp. 81, 90)

canal (cah·*nahl*) bulls' weights are recorded either "en canal" (dressed for butchering) or "en bruto" (whole). The Madrid ring, for example, reports in the newspaper weights "en bruto"; the Málaga ring records the weights "en canal"

capa de paseo (*cah*·pah day pah·*say*·oh) the dress cape (p. 26)

capote (cah·*poh*·tay) the big work cape (p. 37)

cargar la suerte (cahr·*gahr* lah soo·*ware*·tay) following through a pass (p. 45)

carioca (cah·ree·*oh*·cah) maneuver by picador in which he keeps circling the bull as he pics it, thus blocking its exit to the torero making the *quite* and hence submitting it to excessive punishment

cartel (cahr·*tayl*) the colorful posters announcing the fight (p. 33); also means a bullfighter's prestige, as, "He has lots of cartel in Mexico but he's considered a bum in Peru"

casta (*cah*·stah) refers to the high breeding of the bull

castoreño (cah·stohr·*rayn*·yoh) picador's big-brimmed hat

catedral (cah·tay·*thral*) literally, "cathedral" —a very large bull

chicuelina (cheek·well·*ee*·nah) cape pass (p. 66)

chiquero (cheek·*kay*·roh) stall where bull awaits entrance into arena

churumbel (choo·room·*bayl*) gypsy for "kid"

citar (see·*tahr*) to incite bull to charge

clarines (clahr·*een*·ace) the trumpets

cogida (coh·*hee*·thah) a tossing, not necessarily a goring; literally, a catching cojo (*coh*·hoh) lame

coleta (coh·*lay*·tah) pigtail

cornada (cohr·*nah*·thah) a horn wound

cornupeto (cohr·noo·*pay*·toh) synonym for bull

correr la mano (cohr·*rayr* lah *mah*·noh) literally, running the hand; prolonging the one-handed passes to fullest extent of one's arm

corrida de toros (cor·*ree*·tha day *tor*·rohs) literally, a running of the bulls, a bullfight; one speaks of going to "una corrida," or simply "a los toros"

cortar la coleta (cohr·*tahr* lah coh *lay*·tah) to cut the pigtail, i.e., to retire

corto y derecho (*cohr*·toh ee day·*ray*·cho) short and straight—from a short distance and straight over the horn: the best way to "enter to kill"

costadillo, pase de (coh·stah·*theel*·yoh, *pah*·say day) a right-handed muleta pass, similar to pase por alto, but made with feet together and turning slightly with bull as it charges; also known as the "pase militar"

cruz (*croos*) the place on the bull where sword should enter (p. 136)

cruzar (croo·*sahr*) to cross with left hand while killing with right (p. 136); also, to cite bull by crossing line of its charge as indicated by angle of its body

cuadrar (cwa·*thrar*) to square the bull for killing (p. 134)

cuadrilla (cwa·*dreel*·yah) the matador's team (p. 25)

cuarteo (cwar·*tay*·oh) method of placing banderillas (p. 85)

delantera (day·lan·*tay*·rah) sword thrust in front of "the cross"

derechazo (day·ray·*chas*·oh) any right-handed pass with the muleta (p. 103)

derribo (day·*reeb*·oh) knocking over animals with blunt lance (p. 18)

desencajonamiento (days·en·cah·hone·ah·mee·*yen*·toh) lovely word meaning the de-crating (p. 22)

desplante (days·*plahn*·tay) a showing-off maneuver (p. 128)

divisa (dee·*bee*·sah) ribbons of the stable (p. 37)

división de opiniones (dee·bee·see·*own* day oh·peen·*yoh*·nays) division of opinions (p. 146)

doblando (doh·*blahn*·doh) the initial cape-work (p. 41)

embestida (em·bays·*tee*·thah) the charge

embestir (em·bays·*teer*) to charge

embolado (em·boh·*lah*·thoh) bull with horns padded or knobbed, as in Portugal

enganchar (en·gahn·*char*) to hook into, as a horn hooks into a man (p. 135)

entrar a matar (en·*trahr* ah mah·*tahr*) to go in for the kill (p. 135)

eral (air·*rahl*) a two-year-old bull

espada (ace·*pah*·thah) sword; synonym for matador

espantada (ace·pahn·*tah*·thah) usually pronounced "espantá" in Andaluz fashion; means sudden frightened unreasonable fleeing from ring, best illustrated by El Gallo, Cagancho, and Procuna (p. 100)

estampa (ace·*tahm*·pah) general appearance of bull, size, coat condition, etc.

estatuario (ace·stah·too·*ah*·ree·oh) statuesque pass (p. 106)

estocada (ace·stoh·*cah*·thah) sword thrust (p. 136)

estoque (ace·*stoh*·kay) bullfighting sword, seldom called espada (p. 37)

estribo (ace·*tree*·boh) white stirrup board circling base of fence which is used to help the man vault the fence

faena (fah·*ayn*·nah) all work done with muleta (p. 95)

faja (*fah*·hah) sash (p. 26)

farol (fah·*role*) a two-handed spinning pass with cape (p. 79); when done with muleta it is with one hand and known as "un afarolado"

fiesta brava (fee·*yes*·tah *brah*·bah) literally, "the brave spectacle," except that "brava" doesn't exactly mean brave in Spanish; perhaps wild or spirited is better, though not exact

filigrana (fee·lee·*grah*·nah) filigree work, adornments to basic cape or banderilla work

firma, pase de la (*feer*·mah, *pah*·say day lah) right-handed pass invented by Granero (p. 108)

fracaso (frah·*kah*·soh) a flop performance

franela (frah·*nay*·lah) flannel, slang for the muleta

fregolina (fray·goh·*lee*·nah) variation of the gaonera; see *orteguina*

ganadería (gahn·nah·they·*ree*·ah) fighting-bull ranch

ganado (gahn·*nah*·thoh) cattle

gaonera (gah·oh·*nay*·rah) pass with the cape (p. 72)

garrapullos (gah·rah·*pool*·yohs) slang for banderillas

garrocha (gah·*roh*·chah) blunt lance (p. 18)

gitano (hee·*tah*·noh) gypsy; some non-gypsies, like Procuna, are referred to as "muy gitano" because of their superstitions and unpredictability

glosopeda or aftosa (gloh·soh·*pay*·thah) hoof-and-mouth disease, the scourge of bull breeders

golfo (*gohl*·foh) tramp, bum; a favorite insult for the performers

golletazo (gohl·ye·*tah*·soh) a sword thrust in neck instead of withers, deserving boos

granuja (grah·*noo*·hah) bum; favorite epithet for a bad torero

herida (air-*ree*-thah) wound

hierro (ee-*yer*·roh) brand; bulls are branded when approximately a year old

hombro (*ohm*·broh) shoulders; "salir en hombros" means to leave on the shoulders of the crowd (p. 147)

hora de verdad (*or*·ah day bare·*thath*) the moment of truth: the kill (p. 135)

hule (*oo*·lay) the rubber sheet covering operating table, hence synonym for infirmary; one says of a cowardly matador, "He's afraid of the hule" (p. 69)

ilidiable (ee·lee·thee·*ah*·blay) unfightable, as with an animal previously fought

inteligente (een·tel·lee·*hayn*·tay) intelligent; the way bribed newspaper critics refer next day to a rather poor faena

izquierda (ees·kee·*yer*·thah) left; con la izquierda means "with the left hand" (p. 122)

jaca (*hah*·cah) horse, nag

jalear (hah·lay·*ahr*) to encourage bullfighter by shouting

jinete (hee·*nay*·tay) horseman; synonym for picador

lámina (*lah*·mee·nah) same as estampa

lance (*lahn*·say) another word for pass

larga cambiada (*lahr*·gah cahm·bee·*ah*·thah) one-handed pass with the cape (p. 81)

latín (lah·*teen*) an extremely smart bull, usually one fought before, is said to "saber latín"—to know so much he even understands Latin

leña (*layn*·yah) literally, wood; slang for horns

liar (lee·*ahr*) to furl the muleta (p. 135)

lidia (*lee*·thee·ah) combat, as in "toros de lidia"

ligar (lee·*gahr*) to link passes together

limpio (*leem*·pee·oh) clean, an animal never fought before (p. 20)

lío (*lee*·oh) snarled-up mess, impasse, badly directed fight

llena (*yay*·nah) full; term used for a pregnant heifer

llenazo (yay·*nah*·soh) a full house

localidad (loh·cah·lee·*thath*) one's seat in the stands

luces (*loo*·says) lights, sequins (p. 26)

macho (*mah*·choh) masculine, male; on the ranches heifers are referred to as "las hembras" and bulls as "los machos"

machos (*mah*·chohs) technically, bumps on the montera headgear, as well as all tassels on costume; but los machos have come to refer specifically to tassels on knee strings of the taleguilla (p. 26)

Maestranza (mah·ay·*strahn*·sah) Sevilla's bull ring (p. 33)

maestro (mah·*ay*·stroh) title of respect accorded to matador by his subordinates (p. 82)

mamarracho (mah·mah·*rah*·choh) inept bum; favorite insult of Spanish audiences, along with "maleta" and "sinvergüenza"

mandar (mahn·*dahr*) to control (p. 46)

manejable (mah·nay·*hah*·blay) manageable; applied to bull easily handled

mano a mano (*mah*·noh a *mah*·noh) literally, hand to hand (p. 34)

manoletina (mah·noh·lay·*tee*·nah) muleta pass (p. 119)

manso (*mahn*·soh) tame, as opposed to bravo

manso perdido (*mahn*·soh pair·*dee*·tho) hopelessly tame

mansurrón (mahn·soor·*rone*) same as above

mariposa (mah·ree·*poh*·sah) pass with the cape (p. 82)

matador (mah·tah·*dohr*) killer (p. 24); pronounced "mataó" in Andaluz dialect

media-verónica (*may*·thee·ya bare·*roh*·nee·kah) half-verónica (p. 52)

medios (*may*·thee·yos) center of ring (p. 32)

miedo (mee·*yay*·thoh) fear

metisaca (may·tee·*sah*·cah) a bad sword thrust, where matador puts in sword and then withdraws it without letting go of handle

molinete (moh·lee·*nay*·tay) muleta pass (p. 117)

mona (*moh*·nah) picador's leg armor (p. 28)

moña (*mohn*·yah) button to which pigtail is attached

monosabios (moh·noh·*sah*·bee·yos) literally, wise monkeys; the costumed ring servants whose chief function is to help picador maneuver into position

montera (mohn·*tay*·rah) headgear worn by matadors and banderilleros (p. 26)

morillo (mohr·*reel*·yoh) bull's hump of neck muscle (p. 16)

morlaco (mohr·*lah*·coh) slang for a big bull

morucho (mohr·*roo*·choh) half-breed bull

mozo de estoques (*moh*·soh day ace·*toh*·kays) the sword boy

mugir (moo·*heer*) vocal sounds of either bulls or cows

muleta (moo·*lay*·tah) red flannel cape (p. 37)

muletazo (moo·lay·*tah*·soh) any pass with the muleta

muletero (moo·lay·*tay*·roh) a matador who is particularly renowned for his muleta work

mulillas (moo·*leel*·yahs) the drag mules (p. 145)

multa (*mool*·tah) fine imposed by the presidente upon performers for some infraction of bullfighting rules, most commonly upon picadors for pic-ing after trumpet has sounded the end of that act

nadar (nah·*thar*) literally, to swim; colorful way of describing picador's abandoning a horse about to go down from the bull's charge and grabbing out for the safety of the board fence

natural (nah·too·*rahl*) refers to basic left-handed pass generally, but there is a "natural with the right" (see pp. 103, 122)

nervio (*nair*·bee·yoh) spirit in the bull

noble (*noh*·blay) bull that charges completely honestly, with no tricks

novillada (noh·beel·*yah*·thah) apprentice fight (p. 36)

novillero (noh·beel·*yay*·roh) apprentice fighter (p. 36)

novillo (noh·*beel*·yoh) what the novillero fights

obligar (oh·blee·*gahr*) to crowd a reluctant bull so close it feels forced to charge in self-defense

olé (oh·*lay* or *oh*·lay) roughly, "bravo" (p. 46)

oreja (oh·*ray*·hah) ear trophy (p. 146)

orteguina or fregolina (ohr·tay·*gueen*·nah) variation of the gaonera, in which cape is flipped from one hand to other behind the man's back after each charge; attributed to Luis Freg in Mexico and Domingo Ortega in Spain

orticina (ohr·tee·*cee*·nah) a fancy *quite* pass; variation of the chicuelina, invented by the fine Mexican cape artist Pepe Ortiz

palco (*pahl*·coh) a box seat

palitroques (pah·lee·*troh*·kays) twigs; slang for banderillas

palmas (*pahl*·mahs) applause

palos (*pah*·lohs) sticks, slang for banderillas; after putting in only one banderilla the peón will often excuse himself by saying, "Well, that's the way the sticks are made—one at a time"

parar (*pah*·rahr) to stand still (p. 44)

pareja (pah·*ray*·hah) pair (matadors); there is always a "pareja de moda" in demand (p. 34)

parné (pahr·*nay*) caló (gypsy) for money; other slang terms among toreros for money are porcelana, tela, lana

parón (pahr·*rone*) any pass where bullfighter plants his feet and doesn't move them until after bull has passed

paseillo (pah·say·*eel*·yoh) same as following

paseo (pah·*say*·oh) entrance into arena; what toreros call "the only easy thing in bullfighting" (p. 36)

pata (*pah*·tah) bull's hoof, very rarely awarded to the matador as a trophy (p. 146)

pecho, pase de (*pay*·choh, *pah*·say day) the chest pass (p. 127)

pegajoso (pay·gah·*hoh*·soh) a bull that sticks to the horse it has charged and is reluctant to leave it for the capes

pegar (pay·*gahr*) to stick as with the pic

pelea (pay·*lay*·ah) the combat

peña (*payn*·yah) club; just as there are fan clubs for movie stars in America, there are the "peña Arruza" and "peña Manolete," etc., in Spain and Latin America

péndolas (*payn*·doh·lahs) another term for withers, like agujas

peón (pay·*own*) slang for banderillero

peón de confianza (pay·*own* day cohn·fee·*ahn*·sah) matador's number-one banderillero

pequeño (pay·*kayn*·yoh) small, as in most modern bulls

percal (pair·*cahl*) slang for the capote

perfilar (pair·fee·*lahr*) to profile, as before killing.

pescuecero (pays·cway·*ser*·oh) sword thrust or pic-ing low on the bull's neck

peto (*pay*·toh) mattress-like covering which has been required to protect the horses since 1928 (p. 70)

pezuña (pays·*soon*·yah) hoof

pica (*pee*·cah) picador's lance (p. 37)

picador (pee·cah·*dorr*) the mounted lancer (p. 25)

picar (pee·*cahr*) to pic with the lance

pinchazo (peen·*cha*·soh) ineffectual sword thrust (p. 134)

pinreles (peen·*ray*·lays) gypsy for feet, bull's or man's

piquero (pee·*kay*·roh) another word for picador

pitón a pitón (pee·*tohn* ah pee·*tohn*) horn-to-horn passes (p. 133)

pitos (*pee*·tohs) whistling; indicates disapproval. After the matador has killed, sometimes there is a division of opinions, some booing, others applauding because they think the matador did as well as he could with the animal he drew

plaza de toros (*plah*·sah day *toh*·rohs) bull ring (p. 29)

poder (poh·*dair*) power, of the bull

poder a poder (poh·*dair* ah poh·*dair*) method of placing banderillas, tighter and more dangerous variation of al cuarteo

pomo (*poh*·moh) pummel of the sword

por la cara (pohr lah *cah*·rah) face-fighting; the only way to handle some animals reluctant to make a complete charge, the man taking bull head-on and hiding behind full spread of the cape

porrazo (pohr·*rah*·soh) a strong blow, such as suffered by picador and his mount

presidente (pray·see·*dayn*·tay) the supreme authority in the ring (p. 37)

pundonor (poon·do·*nohr*) honor, a sense of obligation to do one's best always, which bullfighters should but seldom do feel

puntas (*poon*·tahs) tips of the horns, now frequently filed off

puntazo (poon·*tah*·soh) light wound

puntilla (poon·*teel*·yah) dagger used for the *coup de grâce* (p. 37)

puntillero (poon·teel·*yay*·roh) the dagger man (p. 144)

puya (*poo*·yah) point of picador's lance (p.77)

puyazo (poo·*yah*·soh) a pic-ing

quedado (kay·*tha*·thoh) "un toro quedado" refers to bull that either because of exhaustion or its temperament is unwilling to charge

querencia (kay·*rain*·see·ah) bull's arbitrary refuge in the arena (p. 96)

quiebro (kee·*ay*·broh) method of placing banderillas (p. 90)

quite (*kee*·tay) act of taking away, rescue (p. 66)

rabioso (rah·bee·*oh*·soh) furious; the way most men get off the ground after being tossed

rabo (*rah*·boh) bull's tail (p. 146)

rebolera (ray·boh·*lay*·rah) decorative terminating pass with the cape (p. 68)

rebrincar (ray·breen·*cahr*) to buck and jump, as when the bull first enters (p. 44)

recibir (ray·see·*beer*) to kill "receiving" bull's charge instead of advancing to meet it (p. 135)

recorte (ray·*cor*·tay) any pass such as media-verónica (p. 53), where the man turns bull so sharply that it is stopped

redondel (ray·dohn·*thel*) another word for the arena

redondo, pase en (ray·*dohn*·tho, *pah*·say enn) muleta pass, generally a natural with the right hand where bull is led around the man, as opposed to pase de la firma where bull's charge is cut short by the muleta's being snatched from its face as soon as horns have passed the man's legs

rehilete (ray·ee·*lay*·tay) synonym for banderilla

rehiletero (ray·ee·lay·*tay*·roh) synonym for banderillero

rejón (ray·*hone*) javelin used by rejoneador (p. 166)

rejoneador (ray·hoh·nay·ah·*thor*) Portuguese-style fighter; see pp. 158, 166

rejoneo (ray·hoh·*nay*·oh) Portuguese style of fighting (pp. 158, 166)

rematar (ray·mah·*tahr*) to finish a series of passes

remate (ray·*mah*·tay) finishing pass, like the rebolera (p. 68)

remos (*ray*·mohs) legs of the bulls or horses

res (rayss) any bovine

reseñas (ray·*sayn*·yahs) newspaper accounts of the corridas

revendedores (ray·ben·they·*thor*·ace) scalpers of tickets

revolcón (ray·bohl·*cone*) a bowling-over by the bull but not an actual goring

rodillas, de (roh·*theel*·yas, day) pass made on the knees (p. 79)

rondeño (rohn·*theyn*·yoh) pertaining to somber Ronda style of bullfighting as opposed to gay Sevillan school; Belmonte, Manolete, and Litri are examples of rondeño style, while Joselito, Arruza, and Pepe Luis Vásquez are pure sevillano

rosinante (roh·see·*nahn*·tay) slang for picador's horse; derived from Quixote's mount

ruedo (roo·*ay*·thoh) the ring; *El Ruedo*, published in Madrid, is the weekly bullfighting magazine, as avidly read as any movie or sporting magazine in America; the Mexican *El Ruedo* is not nearly so good

sablazo (sah·*blah*·soh) sword slash, term for a bad estocada; also means a loan, to have the bite put on one

sacaís (sah·cah·*ees*) gypsy for eyes, of man or bull

sacar (sah·*cahr*) to take out, as in taking a bull out of its querencia (p. 96)

salero (sah·*lay*·roh) salty; a bullfighter with "mucha sal," has grace, personality, and humor in his performing

salida en hombros (sah·*lee*·thah enn *ohm*·brohs) leaving the ring on shoulders of the crowd (p. 147)

saltar (sahl·*tahr*) to jump, as when bull leaps the fence (p. 56)

sanjuanera (sahn·hwah·*nay*·rah) pass of Luis Procuna (p. 98)

semental (say·mayn·*tahl*) seed bull

serpentina (sayr·payn·*tee*·nah) swirling cape pass (p. 74)

servalavari (sayr·bah·lah·*bah*·ree) gypsy for city of Sevilla, spiritual capital of bullfighting

sevillano (say·veel·*ya*·noh) Sevillan style, see *rondeño*

sesgo, al (*says*·goh, ahl) on the bias; way of placing banderillas when bull is inclined to hug fence

sinvergüenza (seen·bayr·*wen*·sah) shameless one, favorite epithet of audiences for toreros

sobrero (soh·*bray*·roh) substitute bull sent in case one of the other animals is rejected

sobresaliente (soh·bray·sahl·*yen*·tay) when only one or two matadors are on the program, a sobresaliente—substitute fighter—must be on hand to take on the animals in case others are unable to because of wounds

sol (sohl) sunny, inexpensive side of the stands (p. 32)

sombra (*sohm*·brah) shady and more expensive half of ring (p. 32)

sorteo (sohr·*tay*·oh) drawing of lots for the bulls (p. 23)

soso (*soh*·soh) dull

suave (soo·*ah*·bay) the smooth, ideal bull that charges straight and clean

suerte (soo·*ware*·tay) word with variety of meanings in bull ring, chief among them being "luck" and "act." One wishes the torero "buena suerte," one refers to the "suerte of the picador or banderillas," and one refers to placing the bull in position for pic-ing as "poniendolo en suerte" (p. 61). *Suerte* also can take on the meaning of direction; when the matador tries to "exit" between bull and fence after a sword thrust, it is known as killing "suerte contraria" (p. 97)

suprema (soo·*pray*·mah) the act of killing is frequently called "la suerte suprema"

susto (*soos*·toh) sudden fright (p. 100)

tablas (*tah*·blahs) boards, synonym for the fence; also designates outer rim of the ring (p. 32)

taleguilla (tah·lay·*gueel*·yah) trousers to the "suit of lights" (p. 26)

tanda (*tahn*·dah) a set or series of passes (p. 127)

tantear (tahn·tay·*ahr*) first passes of a faena, in which the torero merely tries to size up how the bull is charging

tardo (*tahr*·thoh) slow

taurino (tah·oo·*ree*·noh) pertaining to bullfighting

taurófilo (tah·oo·*roh*·fee·loh) another word for aficionado

tauromaquia (tah·oo·roh·*mah*·kee·yah) science of bull combatting (p. 15)

tela (*tay*·lah) cloth; synonym for the capes

teléfono (tay·*lay*·foh·noh) act of resting one's elbow on bull's forehead (p. 131)

templar (taym·*plahr*) to move cape or muleta very slowly and smoothly (p. 46)

temple (*taym*·play) effect of templar-ing (p. 46)

temporada (taym·pohr·*ah*·thah) the bull season (p. 167)

terciado (tayr·see·*ah*·thoh) un toro terciado refers to a rather small animal

tercio (*tayr*·see·oh) literally, third; refers either to the divisions of the arena (p. 32) or to the three main acts of the fight—the pic-ing, the banderillas, and the death

tentar (tayn·*tahr*) to try out the calves at the tientas

terreno (tayr·*rayn*·noh) terrain, both the bull's and the man's (p. 96)

testuz (tays·*toos*) bull's forehead

tienta (tee·*yen*·tah) testing of the calves, sometimes called a tentadero (p. 18)

tío (*tee*·oh) literally, "uncle," but it has come to mean "guy"; also used to refer to an exceptionally large bull—"Vaya un tío!" What a monster!

tope (*toh*·pay) shield on picador's lance (p. 78)

torazo (toh·*rah*·soh) large bull

torear (toh·ray·*ahr*) to bullfight

toreo (toh·*ray*·oh) the art of bullfighting

toreo de salón (toh·*ray*·oh day sah·*lone*) practicing capework with no bull around; comparable to shadowboxing for a fighter torero (tohr·*ray*·roh) bullfighter, technically including banderilleros, picadors, and matadors; but when one says "He is a great torero," one means matador (p. 24)

toril (tohr·*reel*) place from which bulls come into ring, called by toreros "el portón de los sustos"—the gate of horrors

toros, los (*toh*·rohs, lohs) way most people refer to bullfighting; *Los Toros* is the title of the huge, definitive, 3-volume masterpiece in Spanish by José María de Cossío

traje de luces (*trah*·hay day *loo*·says) "suit of sequins" or "suit of lights," the costume of the banderilleros and matadors (p. 26)

trapío (trah·*pee*·oh) general physical aspect of bull

trasera (trah·*say*·rah) a sword thrust too far back on bull

trastear (trahs·tay·*ahr*) to give a series of muleta passes lining up bull for the kill

trastos (*trah*·stohs) implements for killing: muleta and sword

trincherazo (treen·chay·*rah*·soh) muleta passes (p. 98)

trotón (troh·*tone*) a bull that trots through its charge instead of attacking with full power

tuerto (too·*wer*·toh) one-eyed; a bull with defective vision should be returned to the corrals and substitute brought out in its stead

tumbos (*toom*·bohs) the spills taken by picadors

Undivé (oon·dee·*bay*) gypsy toreros' word for God

utrero (oo·*tray*·roh) animal between two and three years old. The classifications run: eral, two years old; utrero; novillo, three years old; and toro, four years and up

vaca (*bah*·cah) cow

vacada (bah·*cah*·thah) the whole herd on a ranch

vaquero (bah·*kay*·roh) herdsman, cowboy

vara (*bah*·rah) a pic-ing (p. 78)

varetazo (bah·ray·*tah*·soh) a blow with the horn, not a wound

varilarguero (bah·ree·lahr·*gay*·roh) synonym for picador

velas (*bay*·lahss) literally, candles; but can refer to horns when they are long and go up straight

verónica (bay·*roh*·nee·kah) basic cape pass (p. 44)

veroniquear (bay·roh·nee·kay·*ahr*) to pass the bull with verónicas

viaje (bee·*ah*·hay) the trip, direction of bull's charge (p. 97)

viento (bee·*yen*·toh) wind; see *aire*

volapié (boh·lah·pee·*yay*) flying with the feet, the most popular method of killing (p. 135). Invented by Costillares around 1175, it was known as the "estocada a vuelapies" in olden times

volcarse (bohl·*cahr*·say) to throw oneself over the horns when killing

vuelta (boo·*wel*·tah) the lap around ring accorded the successful matador (p. 146)

zancudo (sahn·*coo*·thoh) a bull long of legs

zapatillas (sah·pah·*teel*·yas) matador's pumps (p. 26)

zurda (*soor*·thah) synonym for the left hand

PHOTOGRAPHIC CREDITS

40. Serrano
41. Aracil
42. Weaver
43. Mari
44. Boetticher
   Collection
45. Ruedo
46. Ruedo
47. Ruedo
48. Mari
49. Serrano
50. Ruedo
51. Ruedo
52. Hermes
53. Ruedo
54. Ruedo
55. Ruedo
56. Ruedo
57. Sosa
58. Boetticher
   Collection
59. Rodero
60. Poveda
61. Mayo
62. S. Yubero
63. Wide World
   Photos
64. S. Yubero
65. S. Yubero
66. Martin
67. Mayo
68. Martin
69. Rodero
70. Arenas
71. Jean Howard
72. Cano
73. Martín
74. Ruedo
75. Ruedo
76. Ruedo
77. Amado
78. Mayo
79. Ruedo
80. Baldomero
81. Ruedo
82. Gonsanhi
83. Aracil
84. Chapesto
85. S. Yubero

86. Serrano
87. Gonsanhi
88. Urbina
89. Ruedo
90. Ruedo
91. Vives
92. Mayo
93. Ruedo
94. Ruedo
95. Ruedo
96. Boetticher
   Collection
97. Ruedo
98. Jean Howard
99. Ruedo
100. Mateo
101. Gonsanhi
102. Baldomero
103. Ruedo
104. Cano
105. Baldomero
106. Rodero
107. Mayo
108. Serrano
109. Conrad
110. Mateo
111. Jean Howard
112. Baldomero
113. Ruedo
114. Ortiz
115. Ruedo
116. S. Yubero
117. Ruedo
118. Martin Chivito
119. Rodero
120. Ruedo
121. Ruedo
122. Reynoso
123. Ruedo
124. Rodero
125. Rodero
126. Rodríguez in
   Boetticher
   Collection
127. Mayo
128. Mayo
129. Ruedo
130. J. Galle
131. Mateo

132. S. Yubero
133. Jean Howard
134. Serrano
135. International
136. Reynoso
137. Reynoso
138. Serrano
139. Ruedo
140. Mateo
141. Jean Howard
142. Mateo
143. Reynoso
144. Mateo
145. Gonsanhi
146. S. Yubero
147. Baldomero
148. Rincón Cordobés
149. Baldomero
150. Baldomero
151. Serrano
152. Serrano
153. Mateo
154. Mateo
155. Mateo
156. Ruedo
157. Gonsanhi
158. Garci-Sanchez
159. Ruedo
160. Mayo
161. Ruedo
162. Mayo
163. Trineras
164. Baldomero
165. Baldomero
166. Aracil
167. Aracil
168. Mateo
169. Baldomero
170. Serrano
171. Cano
172. Ruedo
173. Aracil
174. Serrano
175. Baldomero
176. Mayo
177. Mateo
178. Mateo
179. Ruedo
180. Serrano

181. Jean Howard
182. Jean Howard
183. Ruedo
184. Mateo
185. Ruedo
186. Ruedo
187. Mateo
188. Cano
189. Ruedo
190. Ruedo
191. Ruedo
192. S. Yubero
193. Gonsanhi
194. Serrano
195. Ruedo
196. Ruedo
197. S. Yubero
198. S. Yubero
199. Trineras
200. Granata
201. Ortiz
202. Mayo
203. Baldomero
204. Serrano
205. Cano
206. Serrano
207. Serrano
208. Ruedo
209. Serrano
210. Serrano
211. Mateo
212. Rodero
213. Ruedo
215. Mayo
216. Serrano
217. Baldomero
219. Mateo
222. Cecil Beaton—
   Vogue
223. Serrano
227. Serrano
228. J. Galle
229. J. Galle
230. J. Galle
231. J. Galle
232. J. Galle
233. J. Galle
Tailpiece. Baldomero

SPANISH

Flores
Albarrán

Manuel
Arranz

Juan
Belmonte

Juan
Cobaleda

Conde
de la Corte

Domecq
Díez

Salvador
Guardiola

Garro y Díaz
Guerra

Frías
Hermanos

MEXICAN

Ayala

Coaxamalucan

La Laguna

Piedras Negras

La Punta

Rancho Seco